Congressional Quarterly's
Washington Guidebook

Congressional Quarterly's
Washington Guidebook

Congressional Quarterly
Washington, D.C.

Photos: p. 1 - Air Photographics Inc.; pp. 5, 24, 41, 43, 46, 47, 50, 51, 52, 58, 121 (Education), 141, 161 - John L. Moore; pp. 7, 9, 27, 28, 32, 49, 72 - Ken Heinen; pp. 12, 18, 31, 56, 59, 64, 80, 91, 93 - Library of Congress; p. 37 - Gayle Krughoff; p. 40 - Architect of the Capitol; pp. 69, 77, 82, 114, 136, 157 - Michael Jenkins/Congressional Quarterly; p. 75 - Collection of the Curator, Supreme Court of the United States; pp. 83, 89, 101, 110 - The White House; p. 107 - Everett C. Johnson/Folio Inc.; pp. 118, 122, 123 (Interior), 124, 125, 126, 127, 128 - Sue Klemens; p. 121 (Pentagon) - U.S. Air Force; p. 131 - National Building Museum; p. 145 - Steward Bros. Inc., Photographers; p. 187 - James D. Scherlis.

Copyright © 1990
Congressional Quarterly
1414 22nd Street N.W.
Washington, D.C. 20037

All rights reserved. No part of this publication may be reproduced or transmitted in any form or by any means, electronic or mechanical, including photocopy, recording, or any information storage and retrieval system, without written permission from the publisher.

Printed in the United States of America

Library of Congress Cataloging-in-Publication Data

Congressional Quarterly's Washington Guidebook
    p. cm.
    Includes index.
    ISBN 0-87187-570-5
    1. Washington (D.C.)--Description-1981- --Guide-books. 2. Public buildings--Washington (D.C.)--Guide-books. I. Congressional Quarterly, inc.
F192.3.C665 1990   90-36730
917.5304'4--dc20   CIP

Editor: John L. Moore
Production Editor: Colleen McGuiness
Contributors: Margaret Seawell Benjaminson, Mary W. Cohn, Mary Costello, Nancy Kervin, Julie Mattes, Margaret C. Thompson, Ian Todreas
Indexer: Patricia Ruggiero
Cover Design and Paper Sculpture: Paula Anderson

Congressional Quarterly Inc.

Andrew Barnes *Chairman*
Richard R. Edmonds *President*
Neil Skene *Editor and Publisher*
Robert W. Merry *Executive Editor*
John J. Coyle *Associate Publisher*
Michael L. Koempel *Director of Information Services*
Robert E. Cuthriell *Director of Development*

Book Division

Patrick Bernuth *General Manager*

Book Editorial
David R. Tarr *Director, Book Department*
Nancy A. Lammers *Managing Editor*
Brenda W. Carter *Acquiring Editor*
Jeanne Ferris *Acquiring Editor*
Carolyn Goldinger *Senior Editor*
Margaret Seawell Benjaminson *Developmental Editor*
Ann Davies *Project Editor*
Colleen McGuiness *Project Editor*
Jamie R. Holland *Production Editor*
Nancy Kervin *Production Editor*
Ann F. O'Malley *Production Editor*
Jerry Orvedahl *Production Editor*
Linda Brashears *Administrative Assistant*

Book Marketing
Kathryn C. Suárez *Director, Book Marketing*
Jacqueline A. Davey *Library Marketing Manager*
Kimberly B. Hatton *Marketing Coordinator*
Leslie Brenowitz *Administrative Assistant*

Production

I.D. Fuller *Production Manager*
Michael Emanuel *Assistant Production Manager*
Jhonnie G. Bailey *Assistant to the Production Manager*

Contents

Introduction   1
   L'Enfant's Plan of the City   3

Legislative Branch   7
   Capitol   9
   Congressional Office Buildings   43
   Library of Congress   55

Judicial Branch   69
   Supreme Court Building   71

Executive Branch   83
   The White House   85
   Executive Office Buildings   109
   The Vice President's Residence   113
   Departmental Headquarters   117

Capital Attractions   131

Appendix   161

Index   187

Introduction

L'Enfant's Plan of the City

Whether you are here in person or as an armchair traveler, the Capitol's west terrace is the spot where you can best savor the grandeur of Washington and begin to understand its orderly yet sometimes confusing design.

Straight ahead from this vantage point is the wide, tree-lined National Mall, flanked by Smithsonian museums and extending to the distant Washington Monument and, beyond that, the Vietnam Veterans Memorial, the Lincoln Memorial, and the Potomac River.

The center line of the Mall divides the southwest and northwest quadrants of the city. Nearby in southwest, to your left, is an office/hotel complex honoring Major Pierre Charles L'Enfant, the man who saw the future Capitol Hill as "a pedestal waiting for a monument" and who laid out the national capital for President George Washington. L'Enfant Plaza is a stop on one of two Metro subway lines serving Capitol Hill.

To your right in downtown Washington, the White House can be glimpsed about a mile down Pennsylvania Avenue, NW. It would be more than a glimpse if Andrew Jackson had not irascibly plunked down the Treasury building on a site that partially spoils L'Enfant's visual linkage of the legislative and executive branches.

Washington's most popular memorials, galleries, and museums are clustered in this panorama visible from the Capitol's front porch, a modest eighty-eight feet above the Potomac. The open Mall preserves the view, which Congress further protected in 1901 by decreeing that the Capitol Dome must remain the highest point in Washington, limiting other buildings to the equivalent of about thirteen stories.

Behind you in the center of the Capitol is the point from which imaginary lines radiate to divide the quadrants, out North, East, and South Capitol streets, and the Mall. Nearby in northeast is the newly reinvigorated Union Station—a train terminal, a shopping center, and a stop on Metro's Red line.

Also behind you on the other side of the Capitol are the Supreme Court, Library of Congress, and congressional office buildings. (The Capitol itself has no "behind." It has two

Introduction

"fronts," East and West. Most presidential inaugurations took place on the East Front portico until President Ronald Reagan moved them to the West Front in 1981.)

The Capitol sits alone on a city block, its grounds a combination of gardens and parking lots. The terraces still reflect the design created in the 1870s by noted landscape architect Frederick Law Olmsted. On the grounds below the Capitol is the Botanic Garden.

This little swivel-neck tour has taken in the homes of the legislative, executive, and judicial branches—the main attractions in a city of many. If it were not for them, and for Washington's status as the national capital, the other worthwhile sights of the city—such as the cherry blossoms, the Vietnam Veterans Memorial, and the National Air and Space Museum—likely would not be here either. This guidebook is primarily about the former—the historic and official places from which the American experiment in democracy is still being conducted.

L'Enfant's Vision

Before the Constitution was adopted and ratified, Congress met first in New York and then in Philadelphia. The act of July 16, 1790, which shifted the seat of government to "a district or territory . . . on the river Potomac," made it clear that a new city would have to be laid out, sites selected for the government buildings, and the buildings themselves designed and erected.

The task fell to L'Enfant, who had been instructed by Washington to locate the city on the Maryland side of the Potomac. L'Enfant made several tours of the area, studied maps of European cities, and developed his plan. In a letter to Washington June 22, 1791, he called for a rectangular grid of streets intersected by broad avenues radiating from the Capitol and other "principal places."

The president accepted L'Enfant's recommendations and on December 13, 1791, forwarded them to Congress for its consideration. Although Washington had to dismiss L'Enfant in February 1792 because his work was behind schedule, his plans were used in preparing maps of the city. His recommendation of a site for the Capitol, on what was then Jenkins Hill, was retained.

The area had been occupied earlier by a subtribe of the Algonquin Indians, known as the Powhatans, whose council house had been located at the foot of the hill. The original Capitol grounds were a part of Cerne Abbey Manor, owned by Daniel Carroll of Duddington. The land was purchased by the

L'Enfant's Plan of the City

View of the Mall from the West Front of the Capitol

government for twenty-five pounds an acre, the equivalent at the time of $66.66.

The site overlooked swampland and Tiber Creek, a finger of the Potomac. Straightened into a canal and then captured in pipes and buried, the stream still flows under the Mall area.

The Street System

Because it was planned from the start, Washington had an advantage over early American cities where roads and turnpikes followed old trails and streams in no particular pattern. L'Enfant used the blank sheet to put streets and avenues where he thought they made sense for an open and accessible capital.

Washington, a former surveyor, had chosen the hundred-square-mile federal district, which then included land on the Virginia side of the Potomac. The tract resembled a square standing on one edge at Alexandria, with most of the land adjoining Maryland on the northernmost sides. Congress ceded the Virginia portion back to the state in 1846, reducing the District of Columbia to about seventy square miles.

L'Enfant's design called for the judiciary to be suitably distant from both the executive and legislative branches. Although the Supreme Court never moved there, Judiciary

Introduction

Square northwest of the Capitol became the site of other courthouses. The Supreme Court moved from the Capitol to its own building in 1935.

Other parts of L'Enfant's plan, notably the quartering of the city, were implemented over the years. Visitors can easily tell which quarter they are in by looking for NE, SE, SW, or NW on street signs or maps.

Navigation is also made easier by the street grid. Alphabetical streets run east-west, and numbered streets run north-south.

But getting around Washington is not quite that simple, as millions of motorists have learned. First, there is the possible duplication of addresses because of the quadrants. An intersection in NW may have an equivalent in NE. Second, major avenues cut diagonally across every quadrant, enhancing the city aesthetically but confounding strangers in the process. In the northwest area, most of these streets are named for the original states.

Circles or squares named for generals and other war heroes, including Washington, slow traffic where most of the major arteries intersect. In warm weather these tidy urban parks are abloom with flowers and shrubs. Especially in the spring, their beauty more than compensates for the aggravation for motorists that L'Enfant had unwittingly guaranteed two hundred years earlier.

Legislative Branch

Capitol

It was a "pity to burn anything so beautiful," a British officer reportedly said before setting fire to the United States Capitol during the War of 1812. Even then, at an early stage of its development, the seat of Congress was the most striking public building in Washington, D.C. It remains so to this day.

Though it may appear to the first-time visitor to be a unified whole, the Capitol is not one structure but several. The original building has been added to or renovated numerous times over its nearly two centuries of existence, and the process has by no means ended. The most recent renovation—a four-year restoration of the Capitol's West Front, the side that faces the Washington Monument midway down the Mall—was completed in November 1987.

The Capitol is both symbol and building. The profile of its dome is as typically American as the Eiffel Tower is typically French, or the pyramids are typically Egyptian. It is a shrine for perhaps 2.5 million tourists each year. Yet the building is the hub of activity for a few thousand congressional employees, and within its walls the Senate, House, Library of Congress, and Supreme Court have shifted from room to room in a continuing search for adequate quarters.

Designed originally to be a home for the Senate and the House of Representatives, the Capitol was pressed into service by others almost from the beginning. The Library of Congress did not leave until 1897; the Supreme Court stayed until 1935. Presidential inaugurations have taken place inside Capitol chambers and outside the East and West fronts. The bodies of national leaders have lain in state in the Rotunda. A vast collection of art, some of it priceless and some of it worthless, crowds the floors, walls, ceilings, corridors, and rooms of the Capitol.

Important rooms that may be visited by the public without advance notice include the Rotunda, situated under the dome and decorated with statues and large-scale historical paintings, and Statuary Hall, which contains a collection of bronze and marble statues presented by the various states to commemorate distinguished citizens.

Statue of Freedom

Legislative Branch

History and Description

The Capitol, constructed of sandstone and marble in the classic style, rests on an elevated site chosen by George Washington in consultation with Major Pierre Charles L'Enfant, a young French engineer and city planner. L'Enfant at times referred to the proposed building as "Congressional House," but the name "Capitol" appears to have been the popular choice. President Washington and others associated with its planning used "Capitol" from the beginning.

The building contains 16.5 acres of floor space, an area slightly smaller than the White House grounds. The Senate and House occupy opposite ends of the building; the Senate chamber is in the north wing, the House in the south. The Capitol also includes committee chambers, offices, restaurants, repair shops, and other rooms. Tunnels and subways link the Capitol to Senate and House office buildings nearby.

In general terms, the Capitol has undergone four major periods of construction: The first, which included the original design work and early construction, stretched from 1792 to about 1811. The second period, from 1815 to 1829, saw the completion of the originally planned building, which had been halted by the War of 1812. During this period extensive repairs were made to sections of the Capitol destroyed by the British in 1814. The third period, from 1851 to 1892, included erection of the existing wings used by the House and Senate and landscaping of the grounds. The fourth period began in 1949 with extensive repairs to the roofs of the House and Senate wings and included extension of the East Front in 1962. The 1983-1987 West Front restoration did not expand the building and is not considered a fifth construction phase.

Early Construction, 1792-1811

The three commissioners appointed by Washington to oversee development of the city and the public buildings originally had expected L'Enfant to provide designs for the buildings as well as the city. But by early 1792 it had become clear that the commissioners could not rely on L'Enfant for the building designs, and they decided to conduct a public design competition.

There were few trained architects in the United States, and the response to the competition was disappointing. Only fourteen to sixteen designs were submitted. Dr. William Thornton, a physician and inventor, gained the president's approval with a plan submitted after the deadline. Washington praised Thornton's design for its "grandeur, simplicity, and beauty of the exterior."

The winning design called for a stately, three-story build-

> **Visitors Information**
>
> Public tours of the Capitol are offered at no charge between 9:00 a.m. and 3:45 p.m., seven days a week except for Thanksgiving, Christmas, and New Year's Day. Tours start from the central Rotunda at least every fifteen minutes. During the April-August peak season they get under way as often as every two minutes. Free concerts also are performed on the Capitol grounds during the warm-weather months.
>
> Groups and individuals may gain admission to the Senate and House visitors' galleries by applying ahead of time to the member of Congress representing their state or locality. Senate and House gallery passes are not interchangeable, nor do they admit the bearer to special events or to joint sessions of Congress.
>
> No photographs may be taken in the House or Senate chambers or dining rooms. Cameras must be checked before entering the visitors' galleries. Hand-held cameras may be used elsewhere in the Capitol.
>
> The Senate Restaurant is open to the public.
>
> The U.S. Capitol Historical Society, a nongovernmental body, maintains information centers in the building.
>
> The U.S. Botanic Garden is open to the public daily, from 9:00 a.m. to 9:00 p.m. in June through August and until 5:00 p.m. the rest of the year.
>
> The Poplar Point Nursery also is open to the public daily.

ing, surmounted by a low dome. For the design, Thornton received $500 and a lot on North Capitol Street, about two blocks from the building site.

Thornton was an amateur architect, and his design was merely a sketch. The commissioners hired Stephen M. Hallet, a professional French architect whose design entry lost out to Thornton's, to prepare working drawings. A clash was inevitable. As modifications of Thornton's design (some of them required for structural and practical reasons) crept into Hallet's drawings, Thornton raised a series of noisy objections. To settle the dispute, Washington called a meeting of Thornton, Hallet, James Hoban (winner of the design competition for the White House), and two builders. The group agreed to some

Legislative Branch

of Hallet's modifications.

Secretary of State Thomas Jefferson wrote to Washington that Hallet had "preserved the most valuable ideas of the original and rendered them acceptable of execution, so that it is considered Dr. Thornton's plan rendered into practical form." Historians still are uncertain as to which man had greater influence over the Capitol's ultimate design.

The Capitol was laid out on a north-south axis, so that descriptions mention north and south wings (ends) and east and west fronts (sides).

The first cornerstone was laid September 18, 1793, by George Washington amid colorful Masonic rites. Although contemporary accounts put the cornerstone at the southeast corner of the north wing, it was not found during the 1958-1962 extension of the East Front.

Hallet was placed in charge of the construction, under the supervision of Hoban. As work progressed, Hallet persisted in altering the design without approval of either the president or the commissioners. Hallet was tolerated for a year but finally was discharged on November 15, 1794.

Nearly a year passed before George Hadfield, a prize-winning student at the Royal Academy in London, was chosen as Hallet's successor. In the interval, Hoban superintended construction of both the White House and the Capitol.

The original dome of the Capitol, 1846

Capitol

Although Thornton's basic design for the Capitol was executed by three other men—Hallet, Hoban, and Hadfield—only Thornton was appointed by the president to the position that has come to be called "architect of the Capitol."

Meanwhile, construction continued. It took slave labor to build the home of a free government. The Capitol work force was composed in large part of black slaves hired out by their masters in the District of Columbia and nearby Maryland and Virginia, as was then a common custom.

Arrival of Congress

The north, or Senate, wing of the Capitol was finished in 1800. Records, archives, and furniture arrived by ship from Philadelphia, the former seat of the federal government, in October of that year. Congress convened in the Capitol for the first time on November 21, 1800.

President John Adams addressed the members the next day, congratulating them "on the prospect of a residence not to be changed." The Senate then consisted of thirty-two members from sixteen states, while the House of Representatives numbered one hundred five. It was not until 1913 that another president, Woodrow Wilson, came to the Capitol to make a speech to Congress.

Both the House and the Senate were quartered in the north wing because it was the only part of the Capitol that had been completed. The north wing, and the entire Capitol until the 1850s, was built primarily of sandstone from the Aquia Creek Quarry in Virginia. The quarry, on an island in the Potomac about forty miles south of Washington, supplied the stone for all public buildings in the new capital from 1791 to 1837. The soft, light gray "freestone" could be quarried easily and shipped economically to Washington. But it did not wear well and was not used extensively after other quarries came into production. Most of the original sandstone in the Capitol has been replaced or covered over by subsequent construction.

Construction under Latrobe

In 1803 President Jefferson appointed Benjamin Henry Latrobe, an English architect, as surveyor of public buildings and placed him in charge of finishing the Capitol.

After demolition of temporary House quarters on the site (which members called "the oven"), work was resumed on the south wing. The completed north wing determined the exterior design of the south wing, and the completed foundations of the south wing set the form of the interior. But like Hallet and

Legislative Branch

Hadfield before him, Latrobe, as a professional architect, found flaws in Thornton's design. Thornton replied on January 1, 1805, with an open letter to members of the House defending his design. The bitter pamphlet war that ensued rocked Congress and threatened to delay further construction appropriations. Jefferson supported Latrobe, while cautioning him to "deviate as little as possible from the plan approved by General Washington." Latrobe survived the criticism and remained in charge of the work.

The House moved from the north wing into what then was considered its permanent home (later Statuary Hall) for the opening of the Tenth Congress on October 26, 1807. Problems arose almost at once. Latrobe had succeeded in changing Thornton's design for an elliptical House chamber into two semicircles joined by parallel lines, and the acoustics were horrible.

By the winter of 1809-1810, new quarters were ready for both the Senate and the Supreme Court, which had been occupying the old House quarters. The Senate moved from the first floor to its remodeled chamber on the second floor. The Court opened its 1810 term in the first-floor chamber beneath the Senate. Both chambers were used later for other purposes, but for the 1976 Bicentennial they were restored to their appearance of the 1850s.

The threat of an approaching war with Britain began to cut into construction appropriations for the Capitol. Work slowed, then halted. The two sections, the north wing and the south wing, stood apart, separated by the unfinished center section. In 1811, before work was completely suspended, a temporary wooden covered walk was built to connect the two wings.

Reconstruction, 1815-1829

Most of the fighting during the War of 1812 took place far from Washington. But in one of a series of Atlantic seaboard raids a British expeditionary force entered Washington around dusk on August 24, 1814. American troops had put up ineffective resistance, and the town was nearly deserted.

That night a detachment of troops headed by Maj. Gen. Robert Ross and Rear Adm. Sir George Cockburn set the Capitol afire. The building was burned, according to several accounts, after Cockburn had mounted the Speaker's chair in the House chamber and asked, "Shall this harbor of Yankee democracy be burned?" The soldiers shouted, "Aye!" Leaving the Capitol in flames, the troops moved through the city and

> ## Capitol Building Facts
>
> **Site.** On the western end of a plateau known previously as Jenkins Heights, eighty-eight feet above the Potomac River. Located at the intersection of the Mall and North, East, and South Capitol streets.
>
> **Grounds.** Total of about 181 acres, including the Capitol, several congressional office buildings, the Library of Congress, the Supreme Court, and surrounding grounds, sidewalks, and roads.
>
> **Dimensions.** Overall length 751 feet, 4 inches. Greatest width, including approaches, 350 feet. Height 287 feet, 5.5 inches from the East Front base to the top of the Statue of Freedom. The Capitol covers about four acres.
>
> **Capacity.** Floor area of 16.5 acres on five levels. Contains approximately 540 rooms devoted to offices, committee rooms, restaurants, storage, and other purposes. There are 658 windows and 850 doorways.
>
> **Statue of Freedom.** Female figure cast in bronze from plaster original by Thomas Crawford. Height 19.5 feet. Weight 14,985 pounds.
>
> **Dome.** Width at base 135 feet, 5 inches. Made of cast iron. Weight 4,454.6 tons, or nearly 9 million pounds. Receives light through 108 windows.
>
> **Rotunda.** Interior of the dome is 96 feet in diameter. Height 180 feet, 3 inches.
>
> **House Chamber.** Length 139 feet. Width 93 feet. Greatest height 42.5 feet.
>
> **Senate Chamber.** Length 113 feet, 3 inches. Width 80 feet, 3 inches. Greatest height 42.5 feet.

burned the White House and the Treasury building. Later on the night of August 24 a violent rainstorm drowned the flames, preventing complete destruction of the buildings.

Temporary Capitols

As the president and other government officials returned to Washington August 27, the slow work of reconstruction began. On September 17 the president announced that Congress would convene in Blodget's Hotel, which had been taken over previously by the Post Office and the Patent Office. The huge structure, on E Street between Seventh and Eighth streets, NW, was the only government building not burned by

Legislative Branch

the British. It had been built by Samuel Blodget, Jr., one of the competitors for the original Capitol design, but never served as a hotel.

An act of February 15, 1815, authorized the president to accept a $500,000 loan from Washington banks to pay for rebuilding the Capitol. On March 14 Latrobe was recalled to oversee the work.

In repairing the interiors, Latrobe again redesigned the House chamber, making it semicircular but failing to improve its acoustics. He designed the central section west of the Rotunda, and the famous tobacco capitals for columns in the small rotunda on the second floor. For the East Front, Latrobe designed the main portico and exterior steps. The new steps were to lead from the ground level to the second floor, which had become, and remains, the principal floor of the Capitol. *(Floor plans in Appendix)*

Work on reconstruction was well under way when Latrobe became entangled in a dispute with Samuel Lane, who had been named in 1816 to the newly created post of commissioner of public buildings and grounds. Latrobe resigned November 20, 1817.

Meanwhile, Congress had moved from Blodget's Hotel into new quarters. A group of Washington landowners, worried that Congress might move to another city, had raised $25,000 to build a temporary "capitol" at First and A streets, NE. The cornerstone was laid July 4, 1815, and both the House and Senate met in the new building at the opening of the Fourteenth Congress on December 4, 1815. James Monroe's first inaugural took place in front of the so-called Brick Capitol on March 4, 1817. Congress met in the building for two terms. The site today is occupied by the Supreme Court building. *(Inaugural sites, box, p. 22)*

Appointment of Bulfinch

To succeed Latrobe, President James Monroe on January 8, 1818, appointed Charles Bulfinch of Boston, the first American-born architect to hold the position of architect of the Capitol.

Bulfinch completed the reconstruction of the north and south wings, enabling Congress to resume meeting in the Capitol at the beginning of the Sixteenth Congress on December 6, 1819. The Supreme Court already had returned for its February 1819 term.

The principal contribution of Bulfinch was to supervise work on the central section, for which the cornerstone was laid

August 24, 1818. With some modifications, Bulfinch completed the designs of Thornton and Latrobe for the center and the East and West fronts.

In October 1824 the unfinished Rotunda was used for a public reception for the Marquis de Lafayette. Then in his late sixties, the last surviving major general of the American Revolution was greeted as a hero. The same year John Trumbull's four paintings of scenes from the Revolution, commissioned in 1817, were hung in the Rotunda.

The original Capitol dome, much lower than the existing dome and made of wood sheathed in copper, was completed in 1827. The pediment over the east portico, "Genius of America" by Luigi Persico, was completed in 1828. The following year, construction of the original Capitol was at last completed. The office Bulfinch had held since 1818 was abolished June 25, 1829.

The Capitol as completed in 1829 was 351 feet, 7.5 inches long at ground level and 282 feet, 10.5 inches wide. It took thirty-seven years of construction and repairs for the Capitol to achieve its original design, which it was to retain for only twenty-two years.

Expansion, 1851-1892

Neither the House nor the Senate chamber proved to be very comfortable. In addition to the acoustical problems in the House, both chambers were difficult to heat adequately in winter and ventilate in summer.

As the midpoint of the nineteenth century approached, a new problem arose. The two chambers were becoming overcrowded from the increase in the number of members of Congress representing newly admitted states. It was clear that the Capitol would have to be expanded.

A design competition was held and various plans were considered. On June 10, 1851, President Millard Fillmore approved the general outline of a plan submitted by Thomas Ustick Walter, a Philadelphia architect who had designed Girard College, considered to be an outstanding example of the Greek Revival style then popular in America. Walter was sworn in as architect of the Capitol extension on June 11. His accepted design provided for the erection at either end of the old building of two new wings, which have been used by the House (south wing) and Senate (north wing) ever since.

President Fillmore laid the cornerstone for the extension on July 4, 1851, but work soon was halted by a controversy over charges of fraud and poor construction. Investigating committees found the charges groundless, and appropriations

Legislative Branch

The dome under construction, 1868

were resumed in April 1852.

After renewed congressional sniping at Capitol Architect Walter in 1853, President Franklin Pierce on March 23 transferred responsibility for the construction from the Interior Department to the War Department. Secretary of War Jefferson Davis, who as a senator had led the drive for expansion, named Capt. Montgomery C. Meigs of the Corps of Engineers to superintend the construction, and Meigs began a review of Walter's plans.

Meigs's review left Walter's basic design intact but altered the location of the Senate and House chambers within their respective wings. Walter had put the Senate chamber on the east side of the north wing and arranged it so that the senators would sit facing east. The House, in the Walter plan, was to be on the east side of the south wing, arranged so that the representatives would face south. At Meigs's suggestion, Walter redesigned the location of the chambers to place them in the center of their respective wings, with the Senate facing north and the House south.

On December 16, 1867, the House moved into the chamber it occupies today. Not until 1913 were the individual desks or benches replaced by semicircular rows of seats.

Inadequate acoustics remained a problem for the House even when it moved into its new chamber in 1857. Finally, in 1939, a system of microphones and loudspeakers was installed. After years of opposition, the Senate had a public address system installed in 1970.

A delay in receiving certain ironwork held up completion of the north wing in the 1850s so that the Senate was unable to meet in its new chamber until January 4, 1859. The Senate's old desks were moved to the new chamber; new desks were added from time to time as the number of senators increased.

The exterior marble for the two wings came from quarries in Massachusetts, and marble for the columns was quarried in Maryland. One hundred columns, each cut from a single block of marble, were dressed by stonemasons on the Capitol grounds. Granite was used for the foundations. Before this phase of the construction, the Capitol had been built almost entirely of sandstone.

The Present-Day Dome

Although Walter's plans for extending the Capitol had made no provision for replacing the 1827 Bulfinch dome, it soon became apparent that the greatly enlarged building dwarfed the old dome. Consequently, on April 4, 1855, Congress authorized a replacement, and Walter drew up the plans.

The tiered dome Walter designed became the most distinguishing feature of the Capitol. It is a considerable accomplishment of art and engineering. Walter evidently was influenced by the domes of St. Paul's Cathedral in London and St. Peter's in Rome. The entire dome, including the thirty-six columns in its lower section, is made of cast iron painted to match the Capitol's stonework. It consists of inner and outer shells girded and bolted together. It was assembled with the help of an internal crane that Meigs built from the floor of the Rotunda. The dome is more than 135 feet wide at its base, and the Rotunda inside is 96 feet in diameter.

Work on the dome began in 1856 and was completed in 1865. Construction continued during the Civil War because President Abraham Lincoln wanted the expanding Capitol to

Legislative Branch

be "a sign we intend the Union shall go on."

On December 20, 1863, the last section of the Statue of Freedom atop the dome was bolted into place, crowning the Capitol. Originally designed by sculptor Thomas Crawford as "Armed Liberty," wearing a soft cap like that of the freed Roman slaves, the female statue had been modified at the request of Secretary of War Davis.

Walter resigned as architect on May 26, 1865, as a result of a conflict over enlarging the quarters of the Library of Congress, then located near the West Front of the Capitol. An accidental fire in 1851 had destroyed much of the library.

Capitol during the Civil War

Congress, or what was left of it following secession, had adjourned March 3, 1861, the day before Lincoln's inauguration. When the president on April 15 issued a call for seventy-five thousand volunteers after the Confederates attacked Fort Sumter, the Capitol was still vacant. As the requested troops arrived, they were quartered in the building. In all, some fourteen units were bivouacked in the Capitol at one time or another, a total of three thousand troops.

The soldiers called the Capitol the "Big Tent." Mock sessions of Congress were a favorite pastime. Basement vaults were turned into storehouses for firewood, flour, beef, and pork. Heating furnaces were used for cooking food. Committee rooms were lined with firebrick and converted into giant bread ovens. The Capitol itself became a heavily guarded defensive position.

When Lincoln called a special session of Congress for July 4, 1862, the troops were cleared out and the Capitol was given a thorough scouring. After adjournment of Congress on July 17, the Capitol again was temporarily requisitioned as a hospital for the wounded from the Second Bull Run and Antietam battles. About fifteen hundred cots were set up in the corridors, the Rotunda, and the House and Senate chambers. The patients were transferred to other hospitals before Congress returned December 1, and the Capitol once again was cleaned and refurbished.

Olmsted's Landscaping

As major work on the Capitol expansion drew to a close in the late 1860s, the task of landscaping remained. The most prominent landscape architect of the time was Frederick Law Olmsted, the designer of New York City's Central Park. On June 23, 1874, Congress commissioned Olmsted to landscape the Capitol grounds. The results of his work still surround the building.

Initial work on the grounds was carried out from 1874 to 1882. In 1881 additional funds were sought for the grand marble stairway and terraces on the West Front, which Olmsted also designed. Congress approved the request, and work began in 1884. Space beneath the terraces was designed for use as committee rooms. With the landscaping virtually completed, Olmsted resigned in 1885. The final work on the terraces, finished in 1892, was supervised by Architect of the Capitol Edward Clark.

Twentieth-Century Alterations

For seventy years after the dome was completed, little important architectural work was done on the Capitol. The roofs of the old north and south wings over the original Senate chamber and Statuary Hall were reconstructed and fireproofed in 1902. Then in 1940 Congress authorized remodeling of the House and Senate chambers and replacement of their cast iron and glass ceilings with new ceilings of stainless steel and plaster. Temporary supports were installed under the old, weakened ceilings. But work on the new ones was delayed by World War II.

The actual remodeling was carried out from July 1949 to January 1951. The work incorporated architectural designs used by Thornton and Latrobe in the Supreme Court and Statuary Hall sections of the Capitol and in other buildings of the period on which they worked.

East Front Extension

The most controversial recent alteration of the Capitol was the 1958-1962 extension of the East Front. Although an extension had been discussed for years, its approval in 1956 became a major dispute.

When Capitol Architect Thomas Walter designed the wings for the House and Senate and the new dome, he had suggested extending the east central section to make it symmetrical with the west central section and avoid any appearance of inadequate support for the larger dome. Walter wrote in his 1863 report to Congress: "The eastern portion of the old building will certainly be taken down at no very distant day, and the front extended eastward." But the day was more distant than Walter expected.

Finally, in 1955, Congress authorized a 32.5-foot extension that had been proposed a half century earlier by the firm of Carrere and Hastings. At first, there was little discussion.

Legislative Branch

Inaugural Sites

A president may take the oath of office anywhere, and either in public or private.

Beginning with Andrew Jackson in 1829, thirty-five inaugural ceremonies were held outdoors near the East Front portico of the Capitol, which looks out on the Supreme Court and the Library of Congress. Ten inaugurations have taken place inside the Capitol. Seven presidents took the oath privately when they assumed the office during an emergency. Three presidents—Rutherford B. Hayes, Woodrow Wilson, and Dwight D. Eisenhower—took the oath of office in private on the day required by the Constitution, then repeated the oath in public ceremonies a day or two later.

Breaking with custom, Ronald Reagan was inaugurated in 1981 on the West Front of the Capitol overlooking the Mall. His second inauguration on the same site was forced indoors by cold weather in 1985.

Following is a list of public inaugural sites other than the East Front portico of the Capitol:

Year	President	Location
1789	George Washington	Federal Hall, New York
1793	George Washington	Congress Hall, Philadelphia
1797	John Adams	Congress Hall, Philadelphia
1801	Thomas Jefferson	Senate Chamber, Capitol
1805	Thomas Jefferson	Senate Chamber, Capitol
1809	James Madison	House Chamber, Capitol
1813	James Madison	House Chamber, Capitol
1817	James Monroe	Brick Capitol, Washington
1821	James Monroe	House Chamber, Capitol
1825	John Quincy Adams	House Chamber, Capitol
1833	Andrew Jackson	House Chamber, Capitol
1850	Millard Fillmore	House Chamber, Capitol
1909	William Howard Taft	Senate Chamber, Capitol
1945	Franklin D. Roosevelt	South Portico, White House
1974	Gerald R. Ford	East Room, White House
1981	Ronald Reagan	West Front, Capitol
1985	Ronald Reagan	Rotunda, Capitol
1989	George Bush	West Front, Capitol

Contributing to the project's acceptance were the deteriorating condition of the sandstone facing and Congress's need for additional space. Speaker Sam Rayburn, D-Texas (1913-1961), was one of the strongest advocates of the extension.

As public awareness of the impending project grew, however, strong opposition developed. Architectural and historic preservation groups said the East Front should be repaired, not enlarged. They forced a one-day hearing February 17, 1958, before the Senate Public Works Subcommittee on Public Buildings and Grounds. But on February 21 the extension commission ordered the project to go ahead.

Work began in 1958 under the supervision of Capitol Architect J. George Stewart. On July 4, 1959, President Dwight D. Eisenhower laid the cornerstone for the new marble East Front. The old sandstone walls were retained as a part of the interior wall construction. The original stonework and carvings were copied exactly. The work was completed in 1962, although it was far enough along in 1961 for President John F. Kennedy to hold his inauguration at the East Front on January 20.

The East Front extension added one hundred thousand square feet of space to the Capitol's five floors. It provided 102 new rooms, including 54 offices for individuals and committees, reception rooms, dining rooms, and kitchens, document rooms, entrance foyers, additional elevators, and a private corridor for members between the Senate and House wings.

West Front Restoration

As work on the East Front drew to a close in 1962, the question of whether to restore or extend the West Front began developing into perhaps the most controversial construction issue in the Capitol's long history. At the heart of the controversy was a critical problem that had to be addressed: a structural weakness in the west wall of the Capitol's central section.

The last exposed portion of the original Capitol, the wall was constructed of sandstone on the exterior, brick and stone on the interior, and loose rubble in between. The wall bore much of the lateral load of the huge building and for some time it had been moving slightly, perhaps as much as one-fourth of an inch each year. In 1965 the weakest portions of the West Front were shored with heavy timbers.

A storm of congressional protest erupted when details of a proposed 285-room extension were made public in 1966. The objections were based on economic, historical, and architec-

Legislative Branch

The West Front

tural grounds. Architect of the Capitol Stewart, a former representative from Delaware, was criticized almost daily in the House and Senate for his strong advocacy of the extension plan.

The American Institute of Architects said in a special April 1967 report: "The west front of the Capitol can be restored and its structural weaknesses corrected."

Stewart died in office May 24, 1970. President Richard Nixon on January 27, 1971, appointed George M. White as the ninth architect of the Capitol. White became the Capitol's first professional architect since Walter.

After a year-long study of the various proposals, White concluded that an extension was needed. The controversy continued, but it was cooled somewhat in the late 1970s by other issues and Congress's desire not to disrupt the 1976 Bicentennial observances.

By 1983 the advocates of restoration had won out. Congress appropriated $49 million to stabilize the deteriorated masonry. More than thirty layers of paint were removed and more than a thousand stainless steel reinforcing rods were inserted into blocks that were considered safe enough to remain. About one-third of the sandstone was replaced with Indiana limestone. The work was completed ahead of schedule in 1987, finally permitting removal of the shoring and scaffolding that for years had marred the view of the Capitol from the Mall.

Art in the Capitol

A precise count of the Capitol's art collection is impossible because so much of it is part of the building's decoration. The Capitol also has historically important objects such as the House's silver-and-ebony mace, the Senate desk of Daniel Webster, and the couch on which John Quincy Adams died.

The Capitol is filled with outstanding examples of crafts. The building's decoration includes beautiful brasswork, marble staircases, carved wood and etched glass, intricate masonry, bronze railings, crystal chandeliers, and antique furniture.

In the late 1850s the corridors of the House and Senate wings and several Capitol rooms were laid with glazed ceramic tile manufactured in England. The colorful tile patterns are a distinctive interior feature of the Capitol. The Minton tile was removed from most of the House wing in 1924 because it was badly worn and could not be matched. It was replaced by marble tile.

The basic appearance of the Capitol's interior was set by Benjamin H. Latrobe in his eleven years as architect (1803-1811, 1815-1817). Latrobe's unique designs include the tobacco leaf and cornstalk motifs on columns in the small Senate Rotunda and at the entrance of the old Supreme Court chamber. His work was much admired by Thomas Jefferson.

Portraits and Paintings

The Capitol art collection includes portraits of George Washington by Gilbert Stuart, Charles Willson Peale, and Rembrandt Peale. Thomas Sully's paintings of Jefferson and Jackson also are in the Capitol. Francis B. Carpenter's huge painting of Abraham Lincoln reading the Emancipation Proclamation to his cabinet was painted at the White House, where Lincoln himself authenticated details. The walls of the Rotunda are hung with eight large oil paintings, including four scenes from the Revolution by John Trumbull, who served as an aide to General Washington. Another is Robert W. Weiers's scene, "Puritans on Their Way to America."

The Capitol contains many murals, including several by Constantino Brumidi. Emanuel Leutze's dramatic account of the westward migration, painted in 1862, is at the west staircase of the House wing. Beginning in 1970 Allyn Cox and his successor, Cliff Young, painted murals in the House corridors depicting scenes from the nation's past. Young died before completing the work and a new artist was being sought to continue it.

Perhaps no other artist had so great an impact on the Capitol as Brumidi, an Italian immigrant hired in 1855 to decorate the interior. He continued for twenty-five years, and his works can be seen throughout the building. Brumidi's first work was the decoration of a House committee room (H-144) used at the time by the Agriculture Committee. The artist worked in fresco, applying paint to the surface of the plaster in its initial wet state. His murals in this room, "Calling of Cincinnatus from the Plow" and "Calling of Putnam from the Plow to the Revolution," were the first frescoes in the Capitol.

Brumidi's masterpiece in the Rotunda, the symbolic "Apotheosis of Washington," decorates the canopy of the dome. Working in fresco, Brumidi took eleven months to cover 4,664 square feet of concave surface, often lying on his back nearly one hundred eighty feet above the stone floor. He completed the work in 1866. The three-hundred-foot frieze encircling the Rotunda, which Brumidi began in 1877 when he was seventy-two, illustrates events in American history. From the floor fifty-eight feet below, the frieze appears to be a sculptured relief, but it was painted in fresco on a flat surface. When the frieze was about one-third completed in 1879, Brumidi fell from the scaffold. He managed to catch a rope and was rescued, but the shock of the accident led to his death a few months later.

Filippo Costaggini, Brumidi's assistant, continued the work from 1880 to 1888, executing the designs Brumidi had prepared to circle the Rotunda. But either because of poor judgment or by his own planning, a thirty-two-foot gap remained undecorated. A congressional resolution in 1950 provided for completion of the frieze, and Allyn Cox painted three final scenes in 1953. The frieze ends with the birth of aviation in 1903.

Brumidi's interior decoration elsewhere in the Capitol is spectacular. Painting in fresco and in oils, he filled various walls and vaulted ceilings with colorful designs, scrollwork,

Main stairway on the House of Representatives side of the Capitol

Legislative Branch

painted frames, portraits, landscapes, historical scenes, and pictures of plants and animals. His decoration can be seen in the "Brumidi Corridor" and the "Patent Corridor" on the ground floor of the Senate wing, and in the Senate Reception Room (S-213) and the President's Room (S-216), surely among the most elaborate rooms in America.

The east corridor of the House wing, which Brumidi did not have time to decorate, finally was painted in 1973-1974 by Cox, with the aid of Young and John Charles Roach. The artists filled the varied spaces with ornaments in harmony with

The Rotunda

the Capitol's interiors and painted the vaults with scenes depicting the Capitol's history. The last bay of the corridor, where an elevator was installed, was disguised by a simulated vault.

Statues and Other Sculpture

When the House moved into new quarters in 1857 its old chamber was left unused. Congress in 1864 designated it the National Statuary Hall and invited "all the states to provide and furnish statues, in marble or bronze, not exceeding two in number for each state, of deceased persons who have been citizens thereof and illustrious for their historic renown or distinguished civil or military service...."

Rhode Island sent the first statue in 1870, a marble sculpture of Revolutionary hero Nathanael Greene. The room soon was filled with images of statesmen, educators, suffragettes, generals, scientists, Indians, pioneers, and other heroes. The Capitol also has nine statues other than those contributed by states. Their quality varies greatly, but together they form one of the finest and most representative collections of American sculpture.

By 1933 the combined weight of the statues threatened to collapse the floor. Congress limited Statuary Hall to a single statue per state and authorized the placement of others throughout the Capitol. In 1990 Utah was sending a statue of inventor Philo Farnsworth, the "father of television," to the Capitol, leaving Colorado, Nevada, North Dakota, and New Mexico as the only states with one statue in its halls.

The Capitol has about eighty busts, including the heads of six presidents, five chief justices, and two Indian chiefs. An enormous marble head of Lincoln by Gutzon Borglum is in the crypt. There are thirty-seven busts of vice presidents, twenty of them displayed in niches around the Senate gallery. The House gallery is surrounded by large relief medallions of twenty-three great lawgivers, from Hammurabi to Jefferson.

The pediment over the east portico of the Senate wing, "The Progress of Civilization," by Thomas Crawford, was erected in 1863. The north and west porticoes of the Senate wing were completed several years later. The porticoes of the House wing were finished by 1867, but the pediment over the east portico, "The Apotheosis of Democracy" by Paul Wayland Bartlett, was not installed until 1916.

A memorial to the pioneers of women's suffrage was presented in 1921 and is located in the crypt below the Rotunda. Scuptured by Adelaide Johnson, the monument consists

Legislative Branch

of busts of Elizabeth Cady Stanton, Susan B. Anthony, and Lucretia Mott emerging from an eight-ton block of Carrara marble.

Four pairs of cast bronze doors were executed for the major entrances to the Capitol, but only three of them were installed. The best known are at the east entrance to the Rotunda. Designed and modeled in high relief by Randolph Rogers in 1858, the doors are decorated with scenes from the life of Christopher Columbus. In 1863 the doors were installed between the old House chamber and the south wing, but they were moved to the Rotunda entrance in 1871.

The two pairs of doors at the east entrances of the House and Senate wings were designed in 1855-1857 by sculptor Thomas Crawford, who also modeled the Statue of Freedom on top of the dome. The panels of the doors depict events in American history. The Senate doors were installed in 1868, and the House doors in 1905.

The fourth pair of doors, modeled by Louis Amateis and completed in 1910, were designed for the central west entrance of the Capitol. But they could not be installed because the West Front was restored, not extended. They were exhibited first at the Corcoran Gallery of Art and then (1914-1967) at the Smithsonian Institution. The doors today are displayed on the first floor of the Capitol near the crypt.

The Crypt and Washington's Tomb

In the Capitol basement, two stories below the Rotunda, is an area that was intended to serve as a tomb for George and Martha Washington.

Within a few days after Washington's death on December 14, 1799, Congress adopted a joint resolution to honor the first president by placing his body in a special tomb in a section of the Capitol yet to be built. Meanwhile, Washington was buried at Mount Vernon in accordance with the terms of his will. In a letter of December 31, 1799, Martha Washington gave permission to have his body moved to the Capitol.

Interior construction of the Rotunda was completed by 1824, but nearly five years more were needed to finish the entire central section. A circular opening about ten feet in diameter was left in the center of the Rotunda floor, to permit visitors to look down upon a statute of Washington that was to have been placed in the crypt on the first floor. The tomb itself was to be one floor below the statue.

In 1828 the opening in the Rotunda floor was closed, because dampness from the lower levels was damaging the

The mace, traditional symbol of legislative authority

John Trumbull paintings hung in the Rotunda four years earlier. In 1830 a House committee recommended that both Washington and his wife be reinterred in the basement tomb.

As the 1832 centennial of Washington's birth approached, Congress asked John A. Washington, grandnephew of the first president, and George Washington Parke Custis, grandson of Mrs. Washington, for permission to move the bodies to the Capitol. Custis consented but John Washington refused. In 1832 the General Assembly of Virginia also adopted a resolution objecting to reinterment. The bodies have remained at Mount Vernon.

The area for the tomb is used to store the Lincoln catafalque, which serves as a bier when bodies of prominent citizens lie in state in the Rotunda. Besides Lincoln, eight presidents have been so honored: Garfield, McKinley, Harding, Taft, Kennedy, Hoover, Eisenhower, and Lyndon B. Johnson.

The crypt itself contains several pictorial exhibits about the history of the Capitol.

The Mace: Symbol of Authority

The most treasured possession of the House of Representatives is the mace, a traditional symbol of legislative authority. The concept, borrowed from the British House of Commons,

Legislative Branch

had its origin in republican Rome, where the fasces—an ax bound in a bundle of rods—symbolized the power of the magistrates.

The mace was adopted by the House in its first session in 1789 as a symbol of office for the sergeant-at-arms, who is responsible for preserving order on the House floor. The first mace was destroyed when the British burned the Capitol in 1814, and for the next twenty-seven years a mace of painted wood was used.

The existing mace, in use since 1841, is a replica of the original mace of 1789. It consists of a bundle of thirteen ebony rods bound in silver, terminating in a silver globe topped by a silver eagle with outstretched wings. It is forty-six inches high and was made by William Adams, a New York silversmith, for $400.

There have been a number of occasions in the history of the House when the sergeant-at-arms, on order of the Speaker, has lifted the mace from its pedestal and "presented" it before an unruly member. On each such occasion, order is said to have been promptly restored. At other times the sergeant-at-arms, bearing the mace, has passed up and down the aisles to quell boisterous behavior in the chamber.

When the House is in regular session, the mace rests on a tall pedestal beside the Speaker's desk. When the House is sitting as the Committee of the Whole, the mace is moved to a low pedestal nearby. Thus it is possible to tell at a glance whether the House is meeting in regular session or as the Committee of the Whole.

The Centennial Safe

Another unusual object in the Capitol is the Centennial Safe, a gift to the government from Mrs. Charles F. Deihm of New York, publisher of the weekly newspaper *Our Second Century*. More than five feet tall, the safe was displayed at the 1876 Centennial Exposition in Philadelphia and later moved to Statuary Hall.

The safe was closed and locked with a key on February 22, 1879. It was opened July 1, 1976, and displayed during the Bicentennial. It contained photographs of distinguished citizens, autographs, a silver inkstand, and other mementoes.

Capitol Activity

Even when Congress is away, the Capitol is a busy place. But the pace steps up when the House and Senate are in session. Visitors are likely to see well-known senators being interviewed for television, members responding to the bells signaling a floor vote, group photographs being taken on the steps, staffers hurrying on an urgent mission, or groups of visitors like themselves casually strolling around or following a tour guide.

Most of the work of Congress is done in committees and a visit to the House or Senate gallery can be disappointing. Nevertheless, witnessing a live session is usually the highlight of a Capitol tour. Passes from a congressional office are required, and doorkeepers herd visitors in and out of the galleries every few minutes so that everyone gets a brief look.

Coverage by Television

Congress for years resisted live televised coverage of its daily proceedings, fearful that cameras would prompt grandstanding or erode the dignity of its operations. Now common-

Legislative Branch

A Typical Day ...

A typical day in the House of Representatives might go like this:
- The chaplain delivers the opening prayer.
- The Speaker approves the *Journal,* the record of the previous day's proceedings. Often a member will demand a roll-call vote on the approval of the *Journal.*
- After some procedural activities—receiving messages from the Senate or the president and granting committees permission to file reports—members are recognized for one-minute speeches on any topic.
- The House then turns to its legislative business. Virtually every major bill is considered under a rule setting guidelines for floor action. The rule is usually approved with little opposition, but the vote can be the first test of a bill's popularity. Those who want a less restrictive rule, so they can offer amendments, often work with opponents of a bill to defeat the rule.

After the rule is adopted, the House resolves into the Committee of the Whole to consider the bill. The Speaker relinquishes the gavel to a chairman, who presides over the committee.

The debate time is controlled by the managers of the bill, usually the chairman and ranking minority member of the standing committee with jurisdiction over the measure. After time for general debate has expired, amendments that are permitted under the rule can be offered. Debate on the amendments is conducted under a rule that limits to five minutes the time each side can speak. Members may obtain additional time by offering pro forma amendments to "strike the last word."

Voting is by voice (the usual procedure); division

place, the gavel-to-gavel broadcasts of floor action have not caused major changes in the way Congress works.

Instead, television coverage has proven politically expedient, as members gain public exposure when national and local news programs air excerpts from floor debates. The broadcasts are also convenient, allowing members to follow floor action from their offices or review a debate they missed. And from them viewers have learned what to expect when seeing a session of Congress, in person or on television. *(How to watch floor*

Capitol

... in the House of Representatives

(members stand to be counted); teller (a seldom-used procedure in which members walk past designated tellers); or by electronic device. When members vote electronically, they insert a plastic card into one of many voting stations on the House floor and press a button to record a "yea," a "nay," or a "present." Their vote is immediately recorded on a big screen on the wall above the Speaker's desk and tabulated, giving a running vote total. Most electronic votes last fifteen minutes.

After the amending process is complete, the Committee "rises," and the chairman reports to the Speaker on the actions taken. Acting again as the House, members vote on final passage of the bill, sometimes after voting on a motion by opponents to recommit the bill to its committee of origin.

• On many noncontroversial bills, the House leadership wants to speed up action, bypassing the Rules Committee and the Committee of the Whole. It can do that by waiving, or "suspending," the rules. Bills under suspension, sometimes as many as a dozen at a time, are usually brought up early in the week. Suspensions cannot be amended. Debate is limited to forty minutes. Then members are asked to vote on whether they want to suspend the rules and pass the bill. A single vote accomplishes both steps. A two-thirds vote is needed to suspend the House rules, making it a gamble sometimes to bring up legislation under suspension. Measures that are even less controversial are placed on the Consent Calendar or are passed by unanimous consent.

• After the House completes its legislative business, members may speak for up to sixty minutes under Special Orders. They must reserve the time in advance but can speak on any topic—often to an almost deserted chamber.

proceedings, box, House, above; Senate, p. 38)

The House was first to open its chamber to television, in 1979. The Senate held out against the television era until 1986. Even senators who once opposed television applauded the results a year later. "It seems to be an unalloyed success at this point.... Our fears were unfounded," said Sen. J. Bennett Johnston, D-La., who had been a vocal opponent. The Senate painted its walls a new color after Kansas Republican Robert Dole complained the old backdrop made senators on TV "look

Legislative Branch

like they're standing in split-pea soup."

Long before broadcasts of floor debate, television had captured dramatic events on Capitol Hill. Presidential State of the Union messages were televised from the packed House chamber. Senate committee hearings were opened to cameras several times, enabling viewers to watch the Kefauver probe of organized crime and the Army-McCarthy investigation in the 1950s, testimony on the Vietnam War in the 1960s, and the Watergate hearings in 1973. The House banned cameras from committee sessions until 1970; in 1974 it won a large national audience for committee sessions on impeachment of President Richard Nixon. In 1987 House and Senate committees jointly held hearings on the Iran-contra affair.

Recordings of House and Senate floor action are not edited. Each chamber, however, does keep close control over its broadcasts, using cameras owned by Congress and operated by congressional staff. The coverage provides only a limited view of floor action, usually focusing on the rostrum or on the member who is speaking.

The cameras are operated by remote control from basement studios under each chamber. Senators speak from their desks; representatives go to one of two lecterns in the House well or use the tables on each side of the central aisle. When votes are in progress, the cameras show the full chamber, with information about the vote superimposed on the screen.

Although networks and local television stations use excerpts from the recordings, the only gavel-to-gavel coverage is on a cable network, Cable Satellite Public Affairs Network (C-SPAN). In addition to its floor coverage, C-SPAN selectively broadcasts other major congressional events—committee hearings, press conferences, and the like. By the mid-1980s more than twenty-three hundred cable systems were carrying C-SPAN, giving Congress a potential audience of 25.5 million households. Only about 9 million of those households received the Senate coverage, however; by the time it was added in 1986 as C-SPAN II, many cable television networks no longer had a channel available.

Controversy about the broadcasts has been rare. In 1984, however, Speaker Thomas P. O'Neill, Jr., D-Mass., angered a group of militant House Republicans when he ordered cameras to pan the chamber, revealing to the television audience that the fiery GOP speakers were talking to an empty House. (House rules give the Speaker control of the broadcast system.) Now cameras routinely show the House chamber during speeches made under special orders—a period at the end of each day's session when legislators may address the often-deserted chamber.

Security: Constant Challenge

The Capitol has been the scene of bombings and other violence over the years, and security to prevent further incidents is one of the building's most important activities.

Until the 1970s it was possible to enter almost any congressional building without hindrance. But that changed after March 1, 1971, when an explosion caused extensive damage in the Senate wing. Coming at a time of rising opposition to U.S. policies in Vietnam, it resulted in an improved security system for the Capitol and congressional offices.

The blast demolished an unmarked rest room on the ground floor of the original Senate wing, the oldest part of the Capitol, and it damaged six other rooms, including the Senate barbershop. No one was injured.

After the bombing, the Capitol police force was doubled to almost twelve hundred, packages and briefcases were inspected at all entrances to the Capitol and congressional office buildings, and some entrances were equipped with x-ray machines.

Despite these and other precautions, another bombing took place in the Capitol on November 7, 1983. A terrorist group claimed responsibility for the blast, which caused considerable damage near the Senate chamber but caused no injuries.

Today, entrance to the Capitol and related buildings is tightly controlled. Visitors must use designated entrances and pass through metal-detecting magnetometer machines. Purses and other packages must be opened or inspected by x-ray.

Pages: Youthful Messengers

Visitors to the Capitol often see young people in dark blue suits hurrying through the corridors with messages or handing out documents on the House or Senate floor. Called pages, the boys and girls are juniors in high school who attend classes early in the morning and then run errands for Congress the rest of the day. About sixty-five pages work for the House and about thirty for the Senate. They are housed on two floors of a congressional office building.

Pages are patronage appointees. Those nominated by the more senior representatives and senators have the best chance of being selected. Pages serve for at least one semester; some stay for a full year. There is also a summer program for pages. Pages do not work directly for those who appoint them but instead report to the House doorkeeper and the Senate ser-

Legislative Branch

A Typical Day . . .

A typical day in the Senate might go like this:
- The Senate is called to order by the presiding officer. The constitutional presiding officer, the vice president, seldom is in attendance. Usually the president pro tempore presides over the opening minutes of the Senate session. During the course of the day, other members of the majority party take turns presiding for an hour at a time.
- The Senate chaplain delivers the opening prayer.
- The majority leader and the minority leader are recognized for opening remarks. The majority leader usually announces the plan for the day's business, which is developed in consultation with the minority leadership.
- Senators who have requested time in advance are recognized for Special Orders; they may speak on any topic for five minutes.
- After special orders, the Senate usually conducts morning business. During morning business—which need not be in the morning—members conduct routine chores. They introduce bills and receive reports from committees and messages from the president.
- After morning business, the Senate considers legislative or executive matters. If the majority leader wants the Senate to begin work on a piece of legislation, the leader normally asks for unanimous consent to call up the measure. If any member objects, the leader may make a debatable motion that the Senate take up the bill. The debatable motion gives opponents the opportunity to launch a filibuster, or extended debate, even before the Senate officially begins considering the bill. A few measures—such as budget resolutions and reports from Senate-House conference committees—are privileged, and a motion to consider them is not debatable.

After the Senate begins work on a bill, floor debate is

geant-at-arms.

By 1988 Congress was paying pages about $850 a month, of which $300 went for room and board (five evening meals a week). Pages are required to follow a dress code. A House description of the page program, noting the extensive walking required on the job, says, "We cannot stress enough that pages bring well broken-in, comfortable shoes."

Congress revamped the page program in the early 1980s

... in the Senate

generally handled by managers, usually the chairman and the ranking minority member of the committee with jurisdiction over the measure. Some measures are considered under a time agreement in which the Senate unanimously agrees to limit debate and to divide the time in some prearranged fashion. In the absence of a time agreement, any senator may seek recognition from the chair, and, once recognized, may speak for as long as he or she wishes. Unless the Senate has unanimously agreed to limit amendments, senators may offer as many as they wish. Generally, amendments need not be germane, or directly related, to the bill.

Most bills are passed by a voice vote with only a handful of senators present. Any member can request a roll call, or recorded vote, on an amendment or on final passage of a measure. Senate roll calls are casual affairs. Few members answer the clerk as their names are called. Instead, senators stroll in from the cloakrooms or their offices and congregate in the well (the area in the front of the chamber). When they are ready to vote, senators catch the eye of the clerk and vote, often by indicating thumbs-up or thumbs-down. Roll-call votes are supposed to last fifteen minutes, but some have dragged on for more than an hour.

- Often, near the end of the day, the majority leader and the minority leader quickly move through a "wrap-up" period, during which minor bills that have been cleared by all members are passed by unanimous consent.
- Just before the Senate finishes its work for the day, the majority leader will seek unanimous consent for the next session's agenda—when the Senate will convene, which senators will be given special orders, and, sometimes, specific time agreements for consideration of legislation.

after criticism that pages were poorly supervised and schooled. Housing for pages, called the Page Residence Hall, was set up in early 1983. Congress also agreed that only juniors in high school should serve as pages; previously pages had ranged in age from fourteen to eighteen, making it difficult to provide an appropriate curriculum. The House began to operate its own school for pages in fall 1983. The Senate opted to extend its contract with the District of Columbia, which once operated

Legislative Branch

both schools.

Scandal twice shook the page program in the early 1980s. In news reports in 1982, two unidentified pages told of sexual misconduct on the part of House members. Later, after a House investigation, they recanted their stories. Joseph A. Califano, Jr., a former cabinet secretary who headed the investigation, said most of the "allegations and rumors of misconduct were the product of teenage exaggeration, gossip, or even out-and-out fabrication that was often repeated mercilessly in a political capital that thrives on rumor."

More painful for the House was its 1983 censure of two representatives who had sexual relationships with pages. Daniel B. Crane, an Illinois Republican with a wife and six children, admitted that he had had an affair in 1980 with a seventeen-year-old female page. Gerry E. Studds, a Massachusetts Democrat, was found to have had a homosexual relationship in 1973 with a seventeen-year-old male page.

Records as early as 1827 show that boys worked as messengers. The name "pages" first appeared a decade later in the *Congressional Globe,* a predecessor of the *Congressional Record.*

Sen. Jacob K. Javits, a New York Republican, appointed the first female page in 1970, but her employment was delayed until the following May, when the Senate voted to permit girls as pages. The House appointed its first girl pages in mid-1973. Javits also broke the color barrier when he appointed the first black page in 1965.

Some pages have returned to the halls of Congress as legislators. Rep. John D. Dingell of Michigan and Sen. David Pryor of Arkansas, both Democrats, were once pages.

Raising the Flags

Much of the Capitol's daily business is conducted in places inaccessible to the casual visitor—on the roof, for instance. It is there that employees of the architect of the Capitol's flag office raise and lower thousands of American flags each year, all destined for shipment to citizens or organizations that request one in writing from their member of Congress.

The flag program began in 1937. By 1990 almost one hundred thousand flags a year—about three hundred a day on average—were being run up a flagpole set aside for that purpose and lowered almost instantly. When mailed, each flag is accompanied by a certificate of authenticity. The recipient is charged a fee pegged to the type of fabric used, cotton or nylon. Each senator and House member may forward as many con-

Capitol

stituent requests as he or she wishes to the flag office.

The all-time record for Capitol flag raising was set on July 4, 1976, the day the nation's Bicentennial was celebrated. On that day 10,471 flags were flown over the Capitol on eighteen temporary flagpoles. Flag raising began at 12:01 a.m. and was concluded at 9:00 p.m.

The flag office also distributes the flags that have flown on the flagpoles located over the East and West fronts of the Capitol. Those flags are flown continuously and are not replaced until they become worn.

Botanic Garden

Flowers and plants for congressional offices are supplied by the U.S. Botanic Garden, which stands at the foot of Capitol Hill. The glass-roofed conservatory collects, cultivates, and grows various plants for public display and for study by students, scientists, and garden clubs. It grows plants and flowers, shrubs, and certain trees for the Capitol grounds. The garden also provides cut flowers and potted plants for congressional offices and public ceremonies. It sponsors several annual flower shows and conducts group tours and horticulture classes.

The U.S. Botanic Garden was founded in 1820 under auspices of the Columbia Institute for the Promotion of Arts and Sciences. It was operated by the institute until 1837, when the organization became inactive and the garden was abandoned.

In 1842 the government had to accommodate the botanical collections brought to Washington from the South Seas by

Legislative Branch

the U.S. Exploring Expedition of 1838-1842, led by Capt. Charles Wilkes. The collections were housed temporarily in the Patent Office but soon were moved to a greenhouse behind the building. The Joint Committee on the Library named the commissioner of patents to oversee the collections.

In 1850 the Botanic Garden was moved to the west end of the Capitol grounds. It was relocated to its current site in 1933 when the conservatory was completed. It did not come under the specific direction of the Joint Committee on the Library until 1856. Today, the committee exercises its supervision through the architect of the Capitol, who has served since 1934 as acting director of the Botanic Garden.

The conservatory is located between Independence and Maryland avenues at First Street, SW. Its large rooms simulate a variety of climates for plant growth.

Directly across Independence Avenue, the garden maintains a one-acre park, which has at its center the thirty-foot Bartholdi Fountain built for the Philadelphia Exposition of 1876. It was designed by Frederic Auguste Bartholdi, better known as the designer of the Statue of Liberty. The garden also operates the Poplar Point Nursery, a twenty-four-acre arboretum that includes many greenhouses, in southeast Washington.

Congressional Office Buildings

The construction of separate office buildings for senators and representatives is a relatively recent occurrence in the history of Congress. The first congressional office building, built for members of the House, was not ready until 1908. Until then, a member's office consisted of a desk in the House or Senate chamber and a rented room in a Washington boarding house. Files were carried in the member's head or pockets.

The record of change from the traditional situation to the contemporary housing of Congress parallels the growth of Congress itself. For the first hundred years of the Republic, congressional service was at most a part-time occupation. Sessions were short. Standing committees were few. And Washington was both inaccessible and inhospitable, which served to protect members from visits by constituents.

In Washington, if members were not actually on the floor they had virtually no sanctuary, except in their boarding houses. The lobbies just off the chambers provided some relaxation. But the lobbies were open to the public, and favor-seekers took advantage of the chance to buttonhole legislators; hence the term "lobbying."

Pressure for additional office space came first from the congressional committees. As standing committees increased in number in the second half of the nineteenth century, they quickly overflowed the rooms allocated to them in the unfinished Capitol. At times, several Senate committees would meet in separate areas of the Senate chamber.

When Charles Bulfinch was at work on the Capitol's center section early in the century, he erected a temporary building for committees where the House wing now stands. The long wooden building stood for only a few years, until the original Capitol was completed. The expansion of the Capitol by Thomas Ustick Walter in the 1850s provided more committee rooms, and much of the space beneath the terraces built in the 1880s was designated for committees.

The proliferation of committees devoured new space almost as fast as it was provided. Not all of the proliferation was dictated by the press of legislative business. A committee office in the Capitol frequently doubled as a personal office for the

Russell building

Legislative Branch

committee chairman. The committee clerks doubled as a personal staff. This dual role of committees was widely acknowledged and occasionally criticized.

As the committees outgrew the space provided even in the expanded Capitol, additional space was rented in nearby privately owned buildings. By 1891 the Maltby Building, at B Street and New Jersey Avenue, NW, had become known as the Senate Annex, housing eighty-one offices. By the end of the century, use of the converted building had become too inconvenient, if not hazardous because of the danger of fire. The Maltby Building had been condemned as unsafe even before the Senate finally left it.

Features and Functions

The House authorized its first office building in 1903; the Senate, in 1904. Once the precedent had been set, pressure for additional buildings was impossible to resist. Instead of abating, the demand mounted as staffs of members swelled and as committees and their expanded staffs moved out of the Capitol and into the office buildings.

Construction continued on and off for the ensuing eight decades. By the end of the 1980s the House had three office buildings and two annexes. The Senate had three office buildings, but, at least temporarily, it had given up the last of several annexes it used until the third office building was completed in 1982.

The earliest of the office buildings were relatively inexpensive to build, even for their day, and their architectural dignity has worn well. But as inflation and Congress's increasingly acquisitive taste drove up their costs, the structures became more undistinguished in design. The Rayburn Building, particularly, was excoriated as "Mussolini modern."

Despite their outside drabness, however, some of the newer buildings were anything but Spartan workplaces on the inside. For senators and representatives they offered swimming pools, gyms, and other amenities that were unthinkable back when Congress first began seeking more space for work.

But even the early buildings made it easy for members to hasten to the floor for a vote without getting their feet wet. Tunnels connect the six office buildings and in four of the tunnels electric subway cars run directly to the Capitol. Visitors may ride the subway cars when members of Congress have not taken all the seats. *(Capitol subways, box, p. 48)*

Most committees of Congress have space in the office buildings, although a handful have retained rooms in the Capitol. Miscellaneous organizations of members, such as the Dem-

Congressional Office Buildings

> ### Visitors Information
>
> The House and Senate office buildings are open to the public Monday through Friday from 8:00 a.m. to 6:30 p.m., and from 8:00 to 11:00 a.m. on Saturdays. Visitors must use designated entrances. Signs outside restricted entrances direct visitors to the nearest public entrance. To enter Senate office buildings, visitors must pass through metal-detection machines. At all entrances, briefcases, purses, and other packages must be opened and inspected by hand or by x-ray machine.
>
> Most congressional hearings are held in the office buildings on Tuesdays, Wednesdays, and Thursdays. The schedule of hearings and other committee meetings is published daily in the *Washington Post*.
>
> The small Senate Chef cafeteria is located off a hallway connecting the Dirksen and Hart buildings, and larger cafeterias are in the Russell and Dirksen buildings. On the House side, the Longworth and Rayburn buildings have large cafeterias. Public access is limited during the 11:30 a.m. to 1:00 p.m. lunch period.

ocratic Study Group, the House Republican Conference, and various congressional and special interest caucuses all have space in the office buildings.

The buildings also house a number of noncongressional organizations, including branch offices of the U.S. Employment Service and the Civil Service Commission and liaison offices of all the armed forces. Assignment of space in the office buildings is based on a member's seniority.

Senior members anxious to escape visiting constituents and lobbyists in the office buildings often are assigned unmarked hideaways in the Capitol. The development of these Capitol offices is a partial reversion to an era that preceded construction of the first office buildings.

House Office Buildings

For years the House buildings were unnamed and were known prosaically as the House Office Building, or, when a second one was built, as the Old House Office Building and the New House Office Building. When a third building was under construction in 1962, the House decided to label all three. It named each building for the House Speaker in office during a major part of its construction. Thus on January 10, 1962, the

Legislative Branch

original office building was named for Joseph G. Cannon, R-Ill. (1873-1891, 1893-1913, 1915-1923), the second one for Nicholas Longworth, R-Ohio (1903-1913, 1915-1931), and the third building for Sam Rayburn, D-Texas (1913-1961).

The House annexes still bear numbers instead of names. They are House Annex 1, at New Jersey Avenue and C Street, NE, and House Annex 2, at Second and D streets, SW.

Cannon Building

President Theodore Roosevelt participated in cornerstone ceremonies on April 14, 1906, for what was to become the Cannon Building on Independence Avenue between C and First streets, SE. Designed by Carrere and Hastings of New York in beaux-arts style, the building was occupied January 10, 1908. Its total cost was under $5 million.

When it was designed, the Cannon Building was large enough to accommodate the existing House membership. But Congress in 1911 authorized an increase in the size of the House to 435 members (the existing limit), and an additional story was erected on the building in 1913-1914. Overall, the building contains about five hundred rooms. It has a pedestrian tunnel to the Capitol but no direct subway connection.

Cannon building

As part of the Rayburn House Office Building project in the 1960s, the Cannon Building underwent a $5 million remodeling.

Longworth Building

Authorized in 1929, the second building for the House—the Longworth Building—was ready for occupancy April 20, 1933. The eight floors occupied by representatives contain 251 two-room suites and 16 committee rooms.

The Longworth Building is on Independence Avenue, SE, between the Cannon and Rayburn buildings. Allied Architects of Washington designed it in neoclassical style. Its cost was $7.8 million.

Rayburn Building

The Rayburn Building was conceived in controversy and completed in conflict. Its legislative history began in 1955 when the Senate's Dirksen Building was under construction and Speaker Rayburn reminded the House of its own space needs.

With the aid of trusted lieutenants, Rayburn, then seventy-three years old, maneuvered the initial funding through as an "emergency" amendment to a supplemental appropriations bill. Under House rules, appropriations bills are supposed to be

Congressional Office Buildings

limited to providing money for projects authorized by previous legislation, but no new building had been authorized by Congress.

Nevertheless, by the time the supplemental appropriations bill emerged from a House-Senate conference, it provided an initial $5 million for the new House office building. Congress gave its final approval April 20, 1955, and the Rayburn Building project was under way.

The company chosen to design the building was the Philadelphia architectural firm of Harbeson, Hough, Livingston, and Larson. Architect John Harbeson was a friend of Capitol Architect J. George Stewart. He also was a friend of fellow Philadelphian Matthew H. McCloskey, treasurer and chief fund raiser for the Democratic party.

McCloskey's construction firm, McCloskey & Co., was the Rayburn Building's principal contractor by virtue of submitting the lowest bid of $6.66 million for excavation and construction of the foundation. Subsequently, the firm also won the contract for construction of the building's superstructure with a bid of $50.8 million. Stewart's office supervised all construction work.

A three-member building commission headed by Rayburn played an active role in designing the building. Writing in

Longworth building

Legislative Branch

Underground Subway System ...

The Senate and House office buildings are linked to the Capitol by underground tunnels. Subway cars have shuttled from the Senate wing to the Russell Building since 1909 and to the Dirksen Building since 1960. The line was extended to the Hart Building in 1982. The only subway service on the House side operates from the Rayburn Building. The tunnel between the Capitol and the Cannon and Longworth buildings is restricted to pedestrian traffic.

Two Studebaker battery-operated vehicles with solid rubber tires provided the first subway transportation to and from the Russell Building. Faster service came in 1912 with two monorail cars powered by overhead wires. Two redesigned monorail cars, produced at the Washington Navy Yard and put into service in 1920, remained in use until 1961.

A new subway system connecting the Senate office buildings with the Capitol began service in 1960. It consists of four eighteen-passenger electric cars on two-rail tracks. At twenty miles an hour, their running time is forty-five seconds from the Russell Building, sixty seconds from the Dirksen Building, and sixty-five seconds from the Hart Building.

A similar system was installed between the Rayburn Building and the Capitol in 1966. Running time is forty seconds.

Fortune magazine, Harold B. Meyers said that "From the start, the architects had limited scope for exercising discretion in the design.... Every decision of any moment—including the controversial layout of the suites and such accoutrements as the commodious safe in each one—had to be referred to the strongminded, busy members of the commission, with Stewart as intermediary." From the time specifications for the superstructure were drawn until bids were submitted, at least seven costly modifications were made in the plans.

The total cost of the Rayburn Building was obscured by design changes and faulty estimates and because other Capitol Hill construction and renovation projects were going on at the same time. Appropriations exceeding $135 million included the Rayburn Building and its site, remodeling of the Cannon and Longworth buildings, and construction of three underground

Congressional Office Buildings

... Links Office Buildings with Capitol

All Capitol subways operate during working hours when Congress is in session, and the public may ride free if space is available. Members of Congress have first priority in using the cars. When the cars are not running, all tunnels remain open to pedestrian traffic.

garages and House subways. According to the office of the architect of the Capitol, final cost of the Rayburn Building itself was $87.7 million, including land acquisition and furnishings.

Completed and occupied in the spring of 1965, the Rayburn Building is larger than the Capitol itself. When approached from the west along Independence Avenue, it appears to dominate Capitol Hill. It is 720 feet long and 450 feet wide (covering about two blocks) and has fifty acres of floor space on nine stories. It is served by twenty-five passenger elevators, twenty-three escalators, and a subway line to the Capitol.

Primary accommodations include one hundred sixty-nine three-room suites for representatives, nine hearing rooms for standing committees, and sixteen for subcommittees. A typical suite is about fifty-four feet long and thirty-two feet wide.

49

Legislative Branch

Eight of the committee hearing rooms are two stories high, and with a large rostrum that can seat up to forty-one representatives. Committee and subcommittee rooms have anterooms and adjoining staff offices. An underground garage was built for sixteen hundred cars and takes up 42 percent of the building's gross floor space. Health facilities include a fully equipped gymnasium, a twenty-by-sixty-foot swimming pool, and compartments identified as "slumber rooms."

Visitors to the Rayburn Building are struck by its opulence and inefficiency. It contains immense amounts of unusable space, and it features thirteen-foot, nine-inch ceilings in most areas and four long dead-end corridors on the upper floors. Critics have noted that only 15 percent of the gross floor space is used for representatives' offices—the original reason for the building.

Aside from the cost and charges of extravagance, most of the criticism leveled at the Rayburn Building dealt with its style. Built of marble and granite, it is known architecturally as "simplified classic." But critics derided it as "Mussolini modern" and "Texas penitentiary." One critic said it could be defended only militarily.

When the building was completed, *New York Times* architectural critic Ada Louise Huxtable wrote that "Architecturally, the Rayburn Building is a national disaster.

Rayburn building

Congressional Office Buildings

Its defects range from profligate mishandling of 50 acres of space to elephantine esthetic banality at record costs.... It is quite possible that this is the worst building for the most money in the history of the construction art. It stuns by sheer mass and boring bulk...."

Stewart's office issued a long statement in reply to the criticism. It read in part, "Esthetics are often matters of opinion. What one person thinks is beautiful, another finds repulsive, and both could be sincere...."

Senate Office Buildings

Like their counterparts on the House side, the Senate office buildings for many years were called simply the Old and New Senate Office Buildings. On October 11, 1972, they were named for two former leaders of the Senate, the first building for Richard Brevard Russell, D-Ga. (1933-1971), and the second one for Everett McKinley Dirksen, R-Ill. (1951-1969). When a third building was authorized later, it was named in honor of Sen. Philip A. Hart, D-Mich. (1959-1976).

Russell Building

The first office building for the Senate was authorized in 1904. Adapted by Carrere and Hastings from its plans for the Cannon Building, the Russell Building was occupied March 5, 1909. However, the First Street side of the building, along with other alterations, was not completed until 1933. The completed building has three hundred fifteen thousand square feet of floor space, excluding parking. The final cost was under $9 million.

At least part of the Russell Building is familiar to millions of television viewers. Its spacious Senate Caucus Room has been the scene of Congress's most celebrated televised investigations, including the organized crime and Army-McCarthy hearings in the 1950s, the Watergate hearings in the 1970s, and the Iran-contra hearings in the 1980s.

Dirksen Building

Congress authorized the Senate's second building—the Dirksen Building—in 1948, and the site, next to the Russell Building, was purchased and cleared. Eggers and Higgins of New York were retained as consulting architects. But the Korean War delayed groundbreaking until 1955.

The building was ready for occupancy October 15, 1958. It has four hundred nineteen thousand square feet of usable floor space. As part of the project, the subway system to the Capitol was rebuilt and extended. The Dirksen Building was the first of the House or Senate office buildings to exceed

Dirksen building

Legislative Branch

Calder mobile in atrium of Hart building

$10 million, requiring more than $24 million to build. That amount, however, soon paled in comparison with the cost of the next congressional office project, the Rayburn House Office Building.

Hart Building

In 1972 the Senate concluded that the Dirksen Building needed to be expanded. An addition, designated the Hart Building in memory of Michigan's Senator Hart, was authorized. After many delays and revised cost estimates, the building was opened in December 1982 at a cost of about $138 million—making it even more costly than the much-criticized Rayburn Building.

Capitol Architect George White laid most of the blame for the high cost on price inflation during the ten years of planning and construction. "Building a building in the face of an inflationary future is like asking how much a quart of milk is going to cost in five years," he said.

The final plans, approved in late 1975, provided that the building would have five hundred forty-six thousand square feet of usable office space for fifty senators, including rooms with eighteen-foot ceilings for senators' offices, a gymnasium, and a two-story public hearing room with built-in television lights and glass booths for network broadcasters.

But White testified in March 1981 that "major portions" would remain unfinished because of the economies imposed in

Congressional Office Buildings

1979 when senators were fretting about the steadily climbing estimates of the building's cost. Among the features left out of the final contracts were the gym, the rooftop restaurant, and the hearing room specially designed for television coverage.

John Carl Warnecke and Associates assisted White on the project as associate architect. Their conservatively modern design is distinguished chiefly by the open seven-story central atrium ringed by glass-walled offices.

In the center of the atrium is the largest single art work in any of the Capitol buildings—Alexander Calder's massive sheet metal and wire mobile, "Maquette for Mountains and Clouds." Calder, who was born in 1898, died in 1976 after designing the scupture. Friends and associates fabricated it according to his design. The finished work was donated to Congress by the Capitol Art Foundation established by C. Douglas Dillon, Paul Mellon, and Nicholas F. Brady.

Library of Congress

The Library of Congress is housed in three sprawling buildings on Capitol Hill. Each year some 2.5 million people troop through those buildings to use the library or simply to view its architecture or exhibits.

With more than 90 million holdings the library may be the largest in the world. But whether it is the greatest is a matter of opinion. There is no standard measurement of library quality, and in measuring greatness it is difficult to compare the library's treasures, such as Thomas Jefferson's rough draft of the Declaration of Independence or James Madison's notes from the Constitutional Convention, with, for example, the British Museum's two signed copies of the Magna Carta.

But by any measure the Library of Congress's collections are unparalleled and of astonishing variety. Although the library does not acquire every book published, its holdings increase at the rate of ten a minute. Works in more than four hundred sixty languages are owned by the library; about two-thirds of its books are not in English.

Besides the Jefferson and Madison items, the library's most valuable holdings include one of three known perfect copies of the Gutenberg Bible, a set of string instruments made by Antonio Stradivari, a nearly complete set of Mathew Brady's photographs of the Civil War, and the personal papers of twenty-three presidents, from Washington to Coolidge.

History of the Library

When Congress decided in 1800 to transfer the new United States government to Washington, D.C., the legislators set aside $5,000 to buy books and set up a congressional library. London booksellers supplied 152 works in 740 volumes, and the Library of Congress was given a room in the Capitol's north wing.

Most of the books were burned or pillaged in 1814 when British troops attacked Washington. After the war, retired president Thomas Jefferson offered to sell Congress his distinguished collection of more than six thousand volumes. Despite some grumbling from Jefferson's critics, the legislators agreed to pay about $24,000 for the library, pricing each book by size and format. President Madison further boosted the library's

Legislative Branch

status in 1815 by appointing George Watterston as librarian, the first person to hold the position on a full-time basis.

The library suffered from another major fire in 1851, when thirty-five thousand of its fifty-five thousand books were lost. After the Civil War, though, the library benefited from a new, stronger copyright law, passed in 1865. It required anyone applying for a copyright to deposit a copy of the publication in the library.

A major advocate of that law was Ainsworth R. Spofford, who in 1864 began thirty-two years of service as the librarian of Congress. Spofford, a bookseller and publisher, was one of three librarians to serve more than three decades. The others were John S. Meehan (1829-1861), a newspaper publisher, and Herbert Putnam (1899-1939), a professional librarian and member of a family of book publishers.

Others who have served as librarian are John Beckley (1802-1807), Patrick Magruder (1807-1814), George Watterston (1815-1829), John G. Stephenson (1861-1897), John R. Young (1897-1899), Archibald MacLeish (1939-1944), Luther H. Evans (1945-1953), L. Quincy Mumford (1954-1974), Daniel J. Boorstin (1975-1987), and John H. Billington (1987——).

Buildings of the Library

The Library of Congress was housed in the Capitol during most of the nineteenth century. William W. Bishop, librarian of the University of Michigan, writing of the library's expansion under Spofford in the first three decades after the Civil War, remarked: "Dr. Spofford waxed old, and the Frankenstein he had created overwhelmed the Capitol."

Congress, by an act of April 15, 1886, authorized the construction of a separate building for the Library of Congress. In 1888 Gen. Thomas L. Casey, chief of engineers of the U.S. Army, was appointed to supervise the construction. It was designed by John L. Smithmeyer and Paul J. Pelz, but architect Edward Pearce Casey was in charge of the building from 1892, including the interior design.

Jefferson Building

The main Library of Congress building, now called the Jefferson Building, was completed in 1897 at a cost of $6,360,000. It is near the Capitol, filling the block bounded by East Capitol Street, Independence Avenue, and First and Second streets, SE. The library's old quarters in the Capitol were closed in July 1897, and the new building was opened November 1. One million books and pamphlets were transferred in the

Jefferson building

Library of Congress

Visitors Information

The main building of the Library of Congress, named for Thomas Jefferson, is located across from the Capitol on First Street, SE. It is connected by pedestrian tunnels to the auxiliary John Adams and James Madison Memorial buildings.

The library is open every day except Christmas and New Year's Day and attracts some 2.5 million visitors and users each year. The library also offers exhibits, concerts, poetry readings, and lectures.

In 1990 the ornate, domed main reading room was closed for renovation until later in the year. It will house forty-five thousand reference works and desks for 250 readers.

Exhibit areas in the three buildings open at 8:30 a.m. and close at 5:30 p.m. The Madison gallery and the Jefferson Great Hall and lower gallery remain open until 9:30 p.m. Monday through Friday and until 6:00 p.m. on weekends. Some reading rooms are open until 9:30 p.m. weekdays.

The Madison Building cafeteria is open to the public from 8:30 to 10:30 a.m. and 12:30 to 3:00 p.m. Monday through Friday. It is reserved for staff during lunch hours.

An eighteen-minute slide show, *America's Library,* is shown in the main building at fifteen minutes before the hour Monday through Friday. Free guided tours are available at 10:00 a.m., 1:00 p.m., and 3:00 p.m.

Use of hand-held cameras is permitted in public areas. Flash photography is prohibited in the visitors' gallery and reading rooms.

The Capitol South Metro stop on the Blue and Orange lines is across First Street from the Madison Building.

---

intervening period. A system of underground conveyor belts was used to move books and reference material between the library and the Capitol.

The inspiration for the gray granite building was the Paris Opera, built in the 1860s. It is in the ornate style of the Italian Renaissance, decorated more richly inside than out, with stairs, walls, and floors of multicolored marble from Tennessee, Italy, France, and Algeria. It is considered a landmark of public

Legislative Branch

building decoration in the United States. The spectacular Great Hall features staircases of sculpture by Philip Martiny, and the corridors contain murals by John W. Alexander and paintings and a marble mosaic by Elihu Vedder. A clock over the entrance to the main reading room is decorated with sculptured figures representing Father Time and the four seasons.

The main reading room was closed from May 4, 1964, to August 16, 1965, to install new heating and air-conditioning systems and new lighting, to improve the book-carrying machinery, and to build temporary offices in the mezzanine of the great hall and the balconies of the main reading room. The partitions—which obscured much of the library's detailed art work—began to be removed in 1979 as library personnel moved into the new Madison Memorial Building.

Another major renovation of the main reading room, scheduled to be completed in late 1990, was to add 38 more reading desks, for a new total of 250. The room was closed to visitors and users until the work was completed.

Adams Building

The main building, after three decades of use, was filling its available space faster than had been anticipated. Congress in June 1930 authorized construction of an annex immediately east of the main building. Completed in April 1939 at a cost of $9 million, the library annex is of white marble, five stories high with three additional stories below ground and a tunnel to the main building. Bas-relief sculpture on its bronze doors represent twelve historic figures credited with giving the art of writing to their people.

In 1980 Congress changed the names of the two buildings. The main building was designated the Thomas Jefferson Building. The annex, previously known as the Thomas Jefferson Building, became the John Adams Building.

Madison Memorial Building

About twenty years after the annex was occupied, the need for additional space again became evident. By the mid-1950s all bookshelves were filled, even though temporary additions brought the total to 336 miles. L. Quincy Mumford noted that during his twenty years as librarian the collections increased by over 100 percent while library space increased by only 42 percent. By the end of fiscal 1974 the library occupied twelve buildings in Washington, Virginia, Maryland, and Ohio. There was hardly room anywhere for materials or library

Library of Congress

The Great Hall

Legislative Branch

employees, who numbered nearly four thousand by late 1975.

An article in *Parade* magazine in 1975 described some of the problems caused by lack of space: "Each year the Library is inundated with 16 million pieces of printed matter. The staff must sift through this paper avalanche, selecting the 3 or 4 million items judged worthy of admission to its shelves. Each book has to be catalogued, then stack attendants must try to squeeze them into the already overloaded shelves. There hasn't been enough room and the books get piled knee-deep on the floor. People seeking to use the Library may sit hour upon hour in the reading room, often vainly waiting.... Stack attendants freely admit that as many as 30 percent of book requests cannot be filled."

Recognizing the need for additional space, Congress October 19, 1965, authorized $75 million for a building that would serve the double purpose of providing a second annex to the library and memorializing President James Madison. An act of March 16, 1970, raised the authorized expenditure to $90 million. Congress had been stung by architectural criticism of the Rayburn House Office Building, so the 1965 law said that plans for the Madison Memorial Building were to be drawn up "after consultation with the American Institute of Architects [AIA]." But Architect of the Capitol J. George Stewart commissioned the firm of Dewitt, Poor, and Shelton without the knowledge of the AIA consultants.

Congress for years put off appropriating the money to erect the Madison Memorial Building, largely because of the tightness of the budget. There was no ground-breaking ceremony, and the building's cornerstone was not laid until March 8, 1974. After numerous delays the building was dedicated April 24, 1980. Construction funds totaled more than $130 million. In December 1979 the first staff contingent from the Congressional Research Service (CRS) moved into the library's new quarters.

The massive 1.5 million square foot building has nine floors of 5.4 acres each, including two floors underground, and is topped by a terraced penthouse housing mechanical equipment, a restaurant, and executive suites. It has eight reading rooms. The building is connected by tunnels to the two other library buildings on Capitol Hill and to the Cannon House Office Building. With the new structure in operation the three buildings of the Library of Congress covered 64.5 acres of floor space and contained 535 miles of bookshelves, mostly in the Jefferson and Adams buildings. The Madison Memorial Building is used mainly for nonbook storage and offices for CRS and

Library of Congress

Types of Holdings

The 90.5 million items in the Library of Congress collections include a vast array of material, ranging from a Stradivarius to a film reel of *Star Wars*. The library's extensive comic book collection was acquired in its capacity as register of copyrights. The collection includes:

Artifacts, instruments, and mementos
Books in the ordinary sense
Books and magazines in Braille
Books and magazines recorded for the blind
Drawings, etchings, prints, and other graphic representations and designs
Incunabula (books published before 1500)
Manuscripts in scrolls, sheets, notebooks, and codex form
Maps
Microfilms and microfiches
Motion pictures, silent and sound
Music in written and printed notations
Music on phonograph records and cylinders
Music on tapes and wires
Musical instruments
Newspapers, loose and in bound volumes
Pamphlets
Periodicals and magazines
Photocopies and photostats
Photographic negatives, prints, and slides
Posters and broadsides
Processed materials—usually typewritten material reproduced by near-print processes
Speeches, recitations, narratives, poetry, and dramatic performances on film, phonograph records, or tape
Technical reports

other divisions.

Like the Rayburn Building and the Hart Senate Office Building, the Madison Memorial Building has been subjected to considerable criticism on aesthetic grounds. Writing in the March 15, 1980, *Washington Post,* the paper's architectural critic Wolf Von Eckhardt commented, "Its architecture seeks not to please and serve people but to impress them. It seeks simplistic solutions to complex problems. It seeks a massive

Legislative Branch

> ## Outstanding Treasures ...
>
> The Library of Congress has a number of exceedingly rare and valuable possessions among its more than 90.5 million books, manuscripts, recordings, photographs, and other items. Some have been displayed in the library, but most are in fragile condition and must be preserved and stored with great care. The library's major treasures include:
>
> *Gutenberg Bible*—One of three known perfect copies on movable type, completed by 1456. Other Bibles in the library include the manuscript Giant Bible of Mainz (1452) and the Necksei-Lipozc Bible in two illuminated volumes from fourteenth-century Hungary.
>
> *Bay Psalm Book*—One of only eleven copies extant of John Eliot's translation of the Psalms. Published in Cambridge, Massachusetts, in 1640, the book is the first example of printing in North America that has survived.
>
> *Stradivari Instruments*—A set of five stringed instruments made by Antonio Stradivari (1644?-1737). The Julliard String Quartet plays them regularly in concert series at the library.
>
> *Declaration of Independence*—Thomas Jefferson's rough draft of the Declaration in his handwriting, with changes written in by Benjamin Franklin and John Adams. The library also has two copies of the first published edition of the Declaration, printed on the night of July 4, 1776, by John Dunlop of Philadelphia. (The original signed copies of the Declaration and the Constitution are displayed at the National Archives.)
>
> *Madison's Notes*—James Madison's personal notes of debates during the 1787 Constitutional Convention in Philadelphia.

monumentality symbolizing power.... Everything is very slick and in exquisitely bad taste, resembling the lobby of an insurance company headquarters building."

Scope of Holdings   In 1990 the Library of Congress owned more than 90.5 million items. The collections included about 28 million volumes and pamphlets, 37 million manuscript pieces, almost 4 million maps, 6 million volumes and pieces of music, and 13 million movies, videos, prints, and other visual materials. Excluding books deposited in regional libraries for the blind and

... of the Library of Congress

Bill of Rights—One of the original engrossed and certified copies. The library also has George Mason's 1776 draft of the Virginia bill of rights.

Gettysburg Address—Abraham Lincoln's first and second drafts of his Gettysburg Address, written on ruled paper. The Lincoln collection includes his manuscript for the second inaugural address.

Civil War Photographs—A nearly complete set of photographs taken during the Civil War by Mathew Brady. Other photographs in the library's collection include pictures taken during the Great Depression by Walker Evans and others.

Folk Music—The library's Archive of Folk Culture has twenty-six thousand cylinders, discs, and tapes of traditional American (including Indian) and foreign folk music, most of it preserved nowhere else. These are noncommercial archival recordings made in the field by folklorists.

Presidential Papers—The personal papers of twenty-three presidents, from George Washington through Calvin Coolidge. The two million documents include Washington's 1775 commission as commander in chief, James Monroe's journal of negotiations for the Louisiana Purchase, and Woodrow Wilson's penciled draft announcing the 1918 armistice.

Music Manuscripts—Examples from virtually all twentieth-century composers and many earlier masters, including Bach, Beethoven, Haydn, Mozart, Schubert, and the largest collection anywhere of Johannes Brahms's manuscripts. The library also has a copy of the first printed book of music, *Odhecaton,* published by Petrucci in Venice in 1504.

physically handicapped, the library had approximately eighty-two thousand Braille volumes and "talking books." The library's holdings include the nation's largest collection of incunabula (books printed before 1500), many donated by Lessing J. Rosenwald and housed in Jenkintown, Pennsylvania.

The library has the world's most extensive collection of aeronautical literature. It has more than a thousand miniature books, none more than four inches high. In the graphic arts, two highly valued collections are the Joseph Pennell collection of Whistleriana and the Brady Civil War photographs.

Legislative Branch

Main reading room

The library's Russian collection is the largest outside the Soviet Union, and its Chinese and Japanese collections are the largest outside the Orient. The library acquires books from some countries by standing orders with publishers and dealers for every important book published.

However, as the eighth librarian of Congress, Herbert Putnam, wrote in one of his forty annual reports: "The progress of the library which is more significant cannot be expressed in figures. It consists in the gradual perfection of its equipment and of its service, in a development of its collections appropriate to its purpose as a library of research, and in a wider appreciation and acceptance of its functions as a national library, with a duty to the entire country."

Reading Room Symbolism

The main reading room of the Library of Congress, which was to reopen after renovation in late 1990, is one of Washington's showplaces. At the center of the library's original 1897 building, the circular room (actually a modified octagon) is topped by a dome 100 feet across and 160 feet high.

Dividing the room's circumference into eight sections are massive pillars of red-brown marble, which are connected by three tiers of alcoves and balconies. The sections are surmounted by semicircular stained-glass windows decorated with the seals of the forty-five states and three territories that composed the federal Union in the 1890s.

The pillars are topped by statues symbolizing different features of civilized life, and under the arches are statues of historic figures from each field of knowledge. Thus, Science is flanked by Isaac Newton and Joseph Henry, Law by Solon and Chancellor James Kent, Poetry by Homer and Shakespeare, Philosophy by Plato and Bacon, Art by Michelangelo and Beethoven, History by Herodotus and Gibbon, Commerce by Columbus and Robert Fulton, and Religion by Moses and St. Paul.

Above the arches is the library dome. Its lowest section contains 320 blue squares bordered in gold and ivory and containing gold rosettes. Over the squares is a painted collar-like area symbolizing the evolution of civilization, with winged figures corresponding to these countries or periods and their contributions: Egypt, written records; Italy, fine arts; Judea, religion; Germany, art of printing; Greece, philosophy; Spain, discovery; Rome, administration; England, literature; Islam, physics; France, emancipation; Middle Ages, languages; and America, science.

At the top of the dome, above the collar, is a painting on a blue field of a female figure representing human understanding. The murals in the dome are by Edwin Blashfield. The floor of the main reading room contains the central reference desk and will have 38 more desks after renovation, for a total of 250. The room and its alcoves and balconies contain about forty-five thousand reference books.

Legislative Branch

Service to Congress

The library has the dual role of assisting Congress and serving as the nation's library. The librarian of Congress oversees both functions, which are carried out by a staff of more than five thousand. The annual budget exceeds $264 million. The librarian is a presidential appointee, confirmed by the Senate, and reports to Congress and its ten-member Joint Committee on the Library. The thirteenth librarian of Congress, James H. Billington, was appointed in 1987 to succeed another historian, Daniel J. Boorstin.

The task of serving two masters—Congress and the public—puts a strain on the library's capacity, sometimes with almost comedic results. *(Conflict of functions, box, p. 67)*

Members of Congress are the most privileged users of the library. Their requests for books or background information are handled by a separate division, the Congressional Research Service, which receives and answers more than five hundred thousand inquiries from Congress each year.

Located within the Madison Memorial Building is the Congressional Reading Room, with space for about sixty-five users. The reading room staff provides members with individual reference service. Another congressional reading room is located in the Jefferson Building.

Senators and representatives, their families, and specific members of their staffs are among the few who may borrow books from the Library of Congress. Books are delivered directly to congressional offices. On the average, one book goes over to the Capitol every ninety seconds, day and night.

Service to the Public

Any person over high school age may use the Library of Congress's two general reading rooms: the main reading room (which was temporarily closed in 1990) located in the Jefferson Building and another reading room on the fifth floor of the Adams Building. In addition, there are distributed among those buildings and the newer Madison Memorial Building the Law Library and specialized reading rooms for the blind and physically handicapped, and in subject areas including geography and maps, Hispanic material, local history and genealogy, manuscripts, microfilms, music, newspaper and current periodicals, Orientalia, prints and photographs, rare books, science, and Slavic materials.

All are open to the public. Each of the rooms has a catalog, reference collection, and reference librarians to provide assistance. Readers may use computer terminals to search the library's data bases for new titles, for sources of information on a variety of subjects, and for legislative histories.

> ## Conflict of Functions
>
> Sometimes the Library of Congress is tugged in different directions by its twin functions—to serve Congress and act as the national library. On a day in 1949 the following dialogue reportedly took place in the library's main reading room:
> **Irate reader.** "I've been asking for that book for six weeks now, and they keep telling me, 'It's in use—it's in use. Wha'dya mean it's in use?"
> **Joseph Rubin, reference librarian.** "It's being used by a member of Congress."
> **Irate reader.** "A Congressman! Why is a Congressman using it? I thought Congress had its own library!"
> **Rubin.** "You may believe it. They do. And you're in it."

Admission to the reading rooms is free, but materials may not be removed from the library. Books requested by readers are delivered to them in the reading rooms, and readers may use the reference books available on the open shelves without filling in a request slip. The main reading room, undergoing extensive renovation, was scheduled to reopen in late 1990 with a collection of forty-five thousand reference books and desks for 250 readers.

During fiscal 1989, 2,357,229 users and visitors entered the library's Capitol Hill buildings. The three main library buildings display changing exhibits prepared by the Exhibits Office. In recent years subjects of major exhibitions and special exhibits have included U.S. courthouse architecture, news photography, Vienna as an international center for opera in the nineteenth century, and the Belgian war for independence. The Gutenberg Bible is on permanent display in the Great Hall of the Jefferson Building.

The library regularly presents films in the Mary Pickford Theater and, in the Elizabeth Sprague Coolidge Auditorium, concerts, readings, and dramatic performances. The Gertrude Clark Whittall Foundation supports concerts featuring the Stradivari instruments, played for many years by the Budapest String Quartet and currently by the Julliard String Quartet. Other concerts at the library have included the Boehm Quintette, the Contemporary Chamber Players of the University of Chicago, and the New York Chamber Soloists. Readings,

Legislative Branch

lectures, and literary conferences have featured Herman Wouk, Sandra McPherson, Barbara W. Tuchman, and many others.

Hundreds of publications and recordings produced by the library are available to the public. Approximately four hundred publications, based mainly on the library's collections, cover an enormous range of subjects. They include scholarly studies, guides to collections, bibliographies, lectures, checklists and directories, and papers presented at such meetings as the Library of Congress Symposium on the American Revolution.

The library also publishes facsimiles of historic documents, manuscripts, and posters, and a variety of greeting cards and gift items. In addition, the library sells more than one hundred long-playing record albums produced from its vast collection of folk music and other recordings. Fifteen albums of traditional American music were produced for sale in connection with the 1976 Bicentennial observance.

Library publications, albums, and other items may be purchased at the library or ordered by mail from the library or the Government Printing Office. (Free catalogs are available from: Publications Distribution Unit, Central Services Division, Library of Congress, Washington, D.C. 20540.) The free monthly *Calendar of Events in the Library of Congress* describes exhibits, concerts, and other public events at the library.

The Library of Congress provides special services to citizens who are blind, partially sighted, or otherwise physically unable to read conventional printed materials. The library and one hundred sixty cooperating regional libraries throughout the nation have books in raised characters (Braille) and books in large type, "talking books" on discs and tapes, and other recorded aids for the physically handicapped. Record and tape players are provided free. In fiscal 1989 the library circulated more than 20 million disk, cassette, and Braille items to 712,300 persons.

One of the library's major services is the cataloging of books. The library assigns to every book published in the United States, and many published abroad, a catalog number that indicates the book's subject matter. In fiscal 1989 the library cataloged 183,991 titles. Since 1981 the library's manual card catalog has been closed and all book control is computerized.

The library's Copyright Office handles more than six hundred thousand new copyright registrations every year. Many of the books and other works deposited for copyright protection are kept, adding to the permanent collection.

Judicial Branch

Supreme Court Building

Of the federal government's three branches, the Supreme Court has the newest home. Its building in the Greek classical style at 1 First Street, NE—facing the Capitol to the west and the Library of Congress's main Jefferson Building to the south—opened in 1935.

For the first 145 years of its existence, the Court was a tenant in buildings intended for other purposes. It did not move into its own building until 1935. Today, well over half a century later, the Court is still housed in a single building. In contrast to Congress, its neighbor on Capitol Hill, the Court has no annexes, no wings or additional buildings.

From the time it opened, the building has been a subject of praise and equally outspoken criticism. It has been described as both a "marble palace" and a "marble mausoleum." Its admirers speak in terms of structural simplicity, austerity, beauty, and dignity. For them, it is a fitting monument epitomizing the words on the front entrance: "Equal Justice Under Law."

Design and Layout

Visitors to the Supreme Court are allowed to see only the ground floor and part of the first floor. The building was designed so that the justices need not enter public areas except when hearing oral arguments and announcing their opinions.

The first floor contains the courtroom, which is open to visitors when the Court is not in session, and the justices' chambers and conference room. A private elevator connects the justices' office corridor to an underground garage.

Public areas of the ground floor include exhibit halls, a cafeteria, and a gift shop. This floor also contains the public information office, the clerk's office, the publications unit, police "headquarters," and other administrative offices.

The first-floor main entrance opens onto the building's Great Hall—its showcase—and the courtroom at the far end. For the Great Hall, architect Cass Gilbert insisted on Ivory Vein Marble from Spain for the walls and Light Sienna Old Convent marble from the Montarrenti quarry in Italy for the huge columns. The Italian marble was hauled to Knoxville, Tennessee, where finishers made the blocks into thirty-foot

Judicial Branch

columns and shipped them to Washington. Darker Italian and African marble was used for the floor.

Most of the building's floors are oak, and the doors and walls of most offices are American-quartered white oak. Bronze and mahogany were also used. The roof was made from cream-colored Roman tile set on bronze strips over lead-coated copper on a slab of watertight concrete. As author Wesley McCune noted, the "Court might succumb to a political storm, but it will never be driven out by any kind of inclement weather."

The building contains two self-supporting marble spiral staircases from the garage to the top floor. The only other spiral staircases like these are in the Vatican and the Paris Opera.

The architects chose the Corinthian style of Greek architecture because they wanted the Court to blend harmoniously with the congressional buildings on Capitol Hill. The dimensions of the building are 385 feet east and west, from front to back, and 304 feet north and south. At its height, the building rises four stories above ground level.

More than $3 million—almost a third of the total cost—was spent on domestic and foreign marble, the building's primary material. A thousand freight cars were needed to haul the pure Vermont marble for the exterior. Georgia marble flecked with crystal was quarried for the four inner courts, while a creamy Alabama marble was used for most of the walls and floors of corridors and entrance halls.

On the steps to the main entrance are a pair of huge marble candelabra with carved panels representing justice, holding sword and scales, and the "three fates," who are weaving the thread of life. On either side of the steps are two marble figures by sculptor James Earle Fraser. On the left side is a female—the contemplation of justice—and on the right is a male—the guardian or authority of law.

At the entrance is a pediment filled with sculptures representing "liberty enthroned," guarded by "order" and "authority." On either side are groups depicting "council and research." Panels on the main door were sculptured by John Donnelly, Jr., and depict scenes in the development of the law. Along both sides of the Great Hall are busts of former chief justices, heraldic devices, and medallion profiles of lawgivers.

From the Great Hall oak doors open into the courtroom, or court chamber. Measuring eighty-two by ninety-one feet with a forty-four-foot ceiling, the room has twenty-four columns of Italian marble. Overhead, along all four sides of the

Visitors Information

The Supreme Court is open for visitors year-round, Monday through Friday from 9:00 a.m. to 4:30 p.m. Attendance at 2:00 p.m. congressional tours may be arranged through a member's office. Annually, some eight hundred thousand people visit the Supreme Court building. The Court is in session for oral arguments during two-week periods from the first Monday in October until May 1. Arguments are held from 10:00 a.m. to noon and 1:00 to 3:00 p.m. Monday, Tuesday, and Wednesday. Winter sessions are less well attended than arguments in the spring. Photographs of the courtroom may be taken when the Court is not in session.

During the weeks when the Court is not in session, lectures are given by the staff of the Curator's Office every hour from 9:30 a.m. to 3:30 p.m.

On the ground floor there are exhibits, portraits of all former justices, a gift shop, and a cafeteria. In addition, visitors can see a film about the Court in a ground floor room.

room, are marble panels sculptured by Adolph A. Weinman. Directly above the bench are two figures, depicting "majesty of the law" and "power of government." Between these figures is a tableau of the Ten Commandments. At the far left is a group representing "safeguard of the rights of the people" and "genii of wisdom and statescraft." At the far right is "the defense of human rights."

On the wall to the right of incoming visitors are figures of historical lawmakers of the pre-Christian era—Menes, Hammurabi, Moses, Solomon, Lycurgus, Solon, Draco, Confucius, and Augustus. These are flanked by figures symbolizing "fame" and "history." To the left of visitors are lawmakers of the Christian era—Napoleon, Marshall, Blackstone, Grotius, Saint Louis, King John, Charlemagne, Mohammed, and Justinian. They are flanked by figures representing "liberty," "peace," and "philosophy."

The basement of the Supreme Court building contains—in addition to the garage—offices of the facilities manager and shops of the thirty-two electricians, plumbers, painters, air conditioning and heating specialists, and groundskeepers. The basement also houses a carpentry shop, laundry, and police

Judicial Branch

roll-call room.

The second floor contains the justices' dining room and library, the office of the reporter of decisions, the legal office, and law clerks' offices.

On the third floor is the library, paneled in hand-carved oak, and on the fourth floor there is a gymnasium and storage area.

Constitutional Role

Entrusted by the Constitution with "the judicial Power of the United States," the Supreme Court is the world's most influential tribunal. This power is political as well as legal, for the Supreme Court functions as both the nation's highest court of appeals and the ultimate interpreter of the Constitution. Many key parts of the Constitution are vague or ambiguous, leaving room for a wide range of opinions by Court members. As a result, the Court through its rulings has often surpassed the federal government's executive and legislative branches in shaping the course of American politics. Two such rulings among many are *Brown v. Board of Education* (1954), which outlawed racial segregation in public schools, and *Roe v. Wade* (1973), which legalized abortion in most instances.

Supreme Court justices are appointed by the president and confirmed by the Senate. Prior judicial service is not required, although most nominees in recent decades have had such experience. Indeed, some of the most highly regarded justices had never before sat on a court. The list includes five chief justices of the United States—John Marshall, Roger Brooke Taney, Charles Evans Hughes, Harlan Fiske Stone, and Earl Warren.

Cases come before the Supreme Court in three ways. First, the Constitution designates two classes of cases as being in the Court's "original" jurisdiction—in other words, eligible for hearing without prior review by a lower court. Such cases, which account for only a small portion of the total number on the Supreme Court docket, are (1) those in which a state is a party and (2) those involving senior foreign diplomats.

Second, the Supreme Court has authority to hear appeals from the lower federal courts. But while the Court is required by law to hear certain types of appeals, most cases come before it through a writ of certiorari. In seeking such a writ, a litigant who has lost a case in a lower court petitions the Supreme Court to review the case, setting forth the reasons why review should be granted. The Supreme Court, under its rules, may grant a writ of certiorari by a vote of at least four justices—an exception to the rule that all business be controlled by majority

Supreme Court Building

decision. In general, the Court grants certiorari only if the case touches on a question of fundamental public importance. About 90 percent of petitions for certiorari fail to win approval.

Third, the Supreme Court reviews appeals from state supreme courts that present a "substantial federal question." Such questions usually arise when a U.S. constitutional right has been denied in the state courts.

The number of justices on the Supreme Court is fixed by Congress, not the Constitution. Under the Judiciary Act of 1789, Congress created a six-member Court. Congress subsequently varied the Court's size from time to time, but since 1869 the tribunal has consisted of a chief justice and eight

Supreme Court library

Judicial Branch

associate justices. In early 1937 President Franklin D. Roosevelt proposed that Congress add as many as six justices to the Court, in an effort to obtain more favorable rulings on the constitutionality of New Deal legislation, but his attempt to "pack" the Court failed.

The Supreme Court convenes on the first Monday in October of each year. It usually hears oral arguments for two weeks at a time, at two-week intervals, but the schedule may vary. It usually recesses in late June until the following autumn.

On Friday of a week of argument (and Saturday, if need be) the nine justices meet in closed session. At the Friday conference the cases ready for decision are discussed and voted upon. If the chief justice votes with the majority, he assigns the writing of the majority opinion; if the "chief" is in the minority, the senior associate justice voting with the majority makes the assignment. Decisions usually are announced to the public on Mondays, but in recent years the press of business has meant that Tuesdays also have produced a number of important rulings.

Early Quarters Between its first meeting in 1790 and October 7, 1935, when the justices first convened in their current building, the Court held session in about a dozen different places. During the Court's first 145 years, the justices moved, on average, once every 12 years.

Some of the early courtrooms were shared with other tribunals. After the Court moved to Washington in 1801, it held formal sessions in various rooms of the Capitol and, according to some sources, in two taverns as well. Some of the premises provided for the Court in the Capitol have been described by commentators of that time as "mean and dingy" and "little better than a dungeon."

New York City. The Supreme Court first met on February 1, 1790, in New York City, then the nation's temporary capital. The Court held session at the Royal Exchange Building at the intersection of Broad and Water streets in what is now Manhattan's financial district. The courtroom occupied the second floor of the gambrel-roofed, cupola-topped building. There was an open-air market on the first floor, and the courtroom on the second floor was a room sixty feet long with a vaulted ceiling.

The justices stayed in New York for two terms. The first lasted from February 1-10, 1790, and the second for only two days, August 2-3, 1790. There were no cases on the Court's

Supreme Court Building

docket during these two terms, and the justices spent their time at such duties as appointing a Court crier—now called clerk of the Court—and admitting lawyers to the bar.

Philadelphia. Before the end of the second term, Congress had voted on July 16, 1790, to move the capital from New York to Philadelphia. The Supreme Court joined the rest of the federal government there for its next session, which began on February 7, 1791, at Independence Hall, then known as "the State House." With no cases to attend to, the Court adjourned the next day.

When the Court moved to Philadelphia, it was understood that the justices would sit in City Hall, but that building was not completed until the summer of 1791, in time for the Court's August 1791 term. The justices met in the east wing of the new City Hall, which also housed the state and municipal court.

Those courts usually met at times different from the Supreme Court. In March 1796, however, the "Mayor's Court" was scheduled to hold a session in the same first-floor courtroom that the Supreme Court was using. As a result, the Supreme Court vacated the courtroom and held session in the

Judicial Branch

chambers of the Common Council on the second floor.

The Court remained in City Hall until the end of the August 1800 term. City Hall also housed the U.S. Congress, which occupied the west wing, and the Pennsylvania legislature, which met in the central part of the building. The records indicate that while in City Hall the justices often kept late hours to hear oral arguments and that there they began wearing robes for the first time.

Washington. The act of July 16, 1790, which transferred the seat of the federal government from New York to Philadelphia, also provided for a subsequent and permanent move to Washington, D.C. The law specified that the final move would take place on the "first Monday in December, in the year one thousand eight hundred." By that time, enough of the Capitol and the White House had been completed for the government to move. Congress and the president were subjected to considerable criticism because the buildings they were to occupy were labeled too palatial and extravagant for a young democracy.

For the Supreme Court, however, there were no accommodations at all. A House committee in 1796 had pointed out that a "building for the Judiciary" was needed, and in 1798 Alexander White, a commissioner for the federal city, had suggested appropriating funds for one. But two weeks before the Court moved to Washington, it was still seeking a place to conduct its business.

Faced with the imminent convening of the homeless Supreme Court in Washington, Congress on January 23, 1801, passed a resolution providing that "leave be given to the Commissioners of the City of Washington to use one of the rooms on the first floor of the Capitol for holding the present session of the Supreme Court of the United States."

Since only the north wing of the Capitol was ready for occupancy at that time, Congress assigned the Court a small room—twenty-four feet by thirty feet, thirty-one feet high, and rounded at the south end—in the east basement, or first floor, entrance hall. There, the Court held its first session in Washington on February 2, 1801.

By 1807 the north wing of the Capitol was in need of renovation. In a letter to Chief Justice John Marshall on September 17, 1807, Benjamin Henry Latrobe, the architect of the Capitol and surveyor of public buildings, suggested that the Court move "for the next session into the Library formerly occupied by the House of Representatives."

There the Court remained for the February and summer 1808 terms. But as Latrobe indicated in a letter to President

Supreme Court Building

James Monroe on September 6, 1809, "the Library became so inconvenient and cold that the Supreme Court preferred to sit at Long's Tavern" during the February 1809 term. Long's Tavern, where the first inaugural ball was held, was located on First Street, SE, where the Library of Congress now stands.

On February 5, 1810, the Court returned to the Capitol and met in a courtroom especially designed for it. Located in the basement beneath the new Senate chamber, the courtroom was also used by the U.S. Circuit Court and probably by the Orphan's Court of the District of Columbia. The noted Philadelphia lawyer, Charles J. Ingersoll, provided this description of the new courtroom:

> Under the Senate Chamber, is the Hall of Justice, the ceiling of which is not unfancifully formed by the arches that support the former. The Judges in their robes of solemn black are raised on seats of grave mahogany; and below them is the bar; and behind that an arcade, still higher, so contrived as to afford auditors double rows of terrace seats thrown in segments round the transverse arch under which the Judges sit.... When I went into the Court of Justice yesterday, one side of the fine forensic colonnade was occupied by a party of ladies, who, after loitering some time in the gallery of the Representatives, had sauntered into the hall, and, were, with their attendants, sacrificing some impatient moments to the inscrutable mysteries of pleading.
>
> On the opposite side was a group of Indians, who are here on a visit to the President in their native costume, their straight black hair hanging in plaits down their tawny shoulders, with mockassins *[sic]* on their feet, rings in their ears and noses, and large plates of silver on their arms and breasts.

The Court remained in the new courtroom until the British burned the Capitol on August 24, 1814, during the War of 1812. The British are said to have used Supreme Court documents to start the fire. When the Capitol was burned, Congress moved to the temporary Brick Capitol at the site of the present Supreme Court building, and then, during the two years that the Capitol was being restored, to a house rented from Daniel Carroll. That house, which the Court used from February 6, 1815, until July 1, 1816, subsequently became Bell Tavern.

The Court returned to the Capitol for its February 1817 term and occupied an undestroyed section in the north wing until 1819. This is the room that was described as "mean and dingy" and "little better than a dungeon." The Court remained there until the February 1819 term, when its regular courtroom

Judicial Branch

beneath the Senate chamber was repaired.

The courtroom, which the justices were to occupy until 1860, was the object of both praise and criticism. It was on the Court's first day in the restored courtroom—February 2, 1819—that the decision in *Dartmouth College v. Woodward* was announced, a decision that made the Court headline news throughout the country. On the same day that *Dartmouth College* was decided, the *National Intelligencer* reported:

> We are highly pleased to find that the Court-room in the Capitol is in a state fit for the reception of the Supreme Court.... It is ... considerably more agreeable than that which was produced on entering the same apartment, previous to the re-modification of it made necessary by the conflagration of the interior of the Capitol.

Many observers saw the courtroom in a less favorable light. The *New York Statesman,* for example, described it as

> not in a style which comports with the dignity of that body, or which wears a comparison with the other halls of the

Supreme Court chamber in the U.S. Capitol, 1860-1935

Supreme Court Building

Capitol. In the first place, it is like going down cellar to reach it. The room is on the basement story in an obscure part of the north wing. In arriving at it, you pass a labyrinth, and almost need the clue of Ariadne to guide you to the sanctuary of the blind goddess. A stranger might traverse the dark avenues of the Capitol for a week, without finding the remote corner in which Justice is administered to the American Republic.

Other critics made note that the chamber was so small that the justices had to put on their robes in full view of the spectators.

Whatever its shortcomings, the courtroom at least lent a new aura of stability and permanence to the previously peripatetic Court. The Court remained in its basement courtroom for forty-one years, surviving fires in 1851 and 1852. After the Court moved to new chambers in 1860, the courtroom became part of the law library of Congress.

In 1860, with the Civil War imminent, the Court moved from the basement to the old Senate chamber on the first floor of the Capitol. The new courtroom was located on the east side of the main corridor between the rotunda and the current Senate chamber. The large room, with a dozen anterooms for office space and storage, was by far the most commodious and imposing quarters the Court had occupied. The galleries had been removed when the Senate moved to its new chambers, giving the courtroom an aura of spaciousness.

The justices sat on a raised platform behind a balustrade. In back of the balustrade was an arched doorway topped by a gilded American eagle and flanked by ten marble columns. The justices faced a large semicircular colonnaded chamber. The area just in front of the bench was used for the presentation of arguments, and it was ringed by wooden benches for the spectators. There were red drapes and carpets, and busts of former chief justices lined the walls.

Despite the dignity and spaciousness of the courtroom, the adjoining office space was cramped and inadequate. There was no dining hall, for example, and the justices were forced to use the robing room for their meals. The conference room, where the justices met to discuss cases and render their decisions, also served as the Court's library. Because of the reluctance of some of the justices to have the conference room windows open, the room was frequently close and stuffy. The clerk's office was similarly close and cluttered.

None of the justices had individual office space in the Capitol; each had to provide for his own and his staff's working quarters at a time when spacious housing in Washington was

Judicial Branch

difficult to find. Nevertheless, the justices held sessions in these quarters for seventy-five years, with two exceptions. An explosion of illuminating gas on November 6, 1898, forced the Court to hold the November 7 and November 14 sessions in the Senate District of Columbia Committee room. During reconstruction of the courtroom from October to December 9, 1901, sessions were held in the Senate Judiciary Committee room.

The Permanent Home

President William Howard Taft began promoting the idea of a separate building for the Supreme Court around 1912. Taft continued to advocate the construction of a Supreme Court building when he became chief justice in 1921. At Taft's persistent urging, Congress finally relented in 1929 and authorized funds for the building of a permanent dwelling for the Court. During the construction, the Court continued to sit in the old Senate chamber. Its last major decision announced there, at the end of the 1934 term, was that of striking down President Franklin D. Roosevelt's National Industrial Recovery Act.

Architect Cass Gilbert was commissioned to design the edifice and, in May 1929, submitted a plan for "a building of dignity and importance suitable for its use as a permanent home of the Supreme Court of the United States." Chief Justice Taft died in 1930 and Gilbert in 1934, but the project was continued under Chief Justice Hughes and architects Cass Gilbert, Jr., and John R. Rockart, under the supervision of Architect of the Capitol David Lynn.

In laying the cornerstone for the new building on October 13, 1932, Chief Justice Charles Evans Hughes paid tribute to his predecessor, Taft. "This building," Hughes said, "is the result of his intelligent persistence." The site chosen for the Court was the location of the Brick Capitol, which had been used by Congress after the British burned the Capitol in 1814.

When Congress in 1929 authorized $9,740,000 for the construction of the Supreme Court building, it was expected that extra funds for necessary furnishings would have to be appropriated. The final and complete cost, in addition to all the furnishings, was below the authorization, and $94,000 was returned to the U.S. Treasury. It is estimated that replacing the building today would run to well over $100 million.

Executive Branch

The White House

The White House, which rivals the U.S. Capitol for the distinction of being Washington's most revered building, serves three main functions. It is the president's home, the president's office, and one of the city's leading tourist attractions, drawing some 1.5 million unofficial visitors a year. Official guests at dinners and receptions swell the annual total of visitors by about fifty thousand.

The White House, located at 1600 Pennsylvania Avenue, NW, is the oldest federal structure in the nation's capital; its cornerstone was laid in 1792. Called "the President's Palace" in the original plans, the building was designed by architect James Hoban and occupies a site chosen by George Washington.

The White House has been hollowed out and its interior rebuilt twice in its history—after the British burned it in 1814 and from 1949 to 1952 during the administration of Harry S Truman, when the building was found to be structurally unsound. Between 1817 and 1902, however, the White House underwent only minor changes in its structure, although every first family engaged in some degree of redecorating, depending on the generosity of Congress.

Many persons viewing the White House for the first time express surprise at its relatively modest size. The main building, four stories high, is 170 feet long and 85 feet wide. New space has been added over the years, including east and west terraces, the president's Oval Office (originally built in 1909 and moved to a different part of the West Wing twenty-five years later), the East Wing (1942), and a penthouse and a bomb shelter (1952).

The only rooms open for public tours are on the main (ground) floor and the state (first floor). The public entrance is the colonnade at the east end of the White House.

Early Years and Restorations

In November 1800, only four months before his single term in office ended, John Adams became the first president to live in the White House. His wife, Abigail, was not impressed by their new home. The place was "habitable," she wrote to her daughter in Massachusetts, but bells for summoning servants were "wholly wanting to assist us in this great castle." She also complained about the lack of warmth, noting that "wood is not to be had, because people cannot be found to cut and cart it!"

Fourteen years later, during the War of 1812, British troops set fire to the White House as well as to the Capitol. Only a torrential rainstorm saved both buildings from being reduced to total ruin.

Among the items salvaged from the Executive Mansion by Dolley Madison, the wife of President James Madison, was the famed full-length portrait of George Washington by Gilbert Stuart. It is the only object known to have remained in the White House since the Adamses first occupied it.

Restoration of the White House, supervised by Hoban, took three years. To hide unsightly smoke stains, the exterior walls of gray stone were painted white. Even before then, however, the building had been known as the White House. Many years later, when President Theodore Roosevelt had it engraved upon his stationery, the name became official.

The main portion of the White House looks much the same today from the outside as it did when the John Adamses moved in. But the interior has undergone many changes. In 1817, for example, Hoban added twelve new fireplaces. Nonetheless, heating the high-ceilinged public rooms remained a problem even after the addition of a central-heating system in 1853.

Plumbing also was a worry. It was not until 1833, during President Andrew Jackson's second term, that the White House was provided with hot and cold running water. A zinc-lined bathtub was installed around 1855, but the White House still had only one full bathroom when President Benjamin Harrison was inaugurated in 1889.

During the Benjamin Harrison administration, the White House was first wired for electric lighting. This change, plus others in later years, meant that floors and walls were continually being pierced to accommodate new flues, pipes, and wires. All these "improvements" eventually took their toll on the structural stability of the aging building.

Signs of serious trouble became impossible to ignore shortly after World War II. In late 1947 President Truman became increasingly disturbed about vibrations in the floors of certain rooms of the White House family quarters. He ordered engineering surveys that found the White House was in such precarious physical shape that it needed immediate and drastic renovation.

A complete restoration of the White House followed,

The White House

Visitors Information

The White House ranks high on the sightseeing lists of most visitors to Washington, D.C. A free, self-guided tour begins on the ground floor corridor and takes them through the public rooms on the main floor. Visitors are welcome Tuesday through Saturday, from 10:00 a.m. to noon. The White House also is open for such tours on certain major public holidays, including Memorial Day and Labor Day. Because, however, the White House sometimes is closed for official visits or business, you may want to call a day before you plan to visit to be sure it will be open. Photography is not permitted inside the building.

The White House Visitors' Office uses a ticket system to minimize long lines and help visitors schedule their day's activities. On tour days, tickets for that day become available at 8:00 a.m. from a special kiosk on the Ellipse, the grassy area just south of the White House. Each person planning to join the tour must be present to get the free entrance ticket. Each ticket is valid for a particular time that same morning; visitors need not show up at the White House until the time their visit is scheduled. The supply of tickets is limited, but for most of the year the seven thousand usually available each day are enough to accommodate visitors. However, during the crush of the summer tourist season, some ticket-seekers are turned away from the kiosk.

Another route to the White House requires advance planning. Most senators and representatives will arrange for their constituents to take part in special White House tours conducted before 10:00 a.m. on Tuesday through Saturday. Congressional tours differ from public tours in that they are conducted in small groups, are guided, and include several rooms not ordinarily open to the public. Write your senator or representative and request the tour on a specific date.

A special weekend garden tour is scheduled each fall and spring; dates vary from year to year but usually are scheduled for mid-April and mid-October. No tickets are distributed; admission is on a first-come, first-serve basis.

The White House Historical Association—740 Jackson Place, NW, one block from the White House—sells literature about the White House and Washington, D.C.

Executive Branch

lasting from late 1949 to early 1952. During that time, the Trumans lived at Blair House, just across Pennsylvania Avenue from the White House. In their absence the Executive Mansion's original exterior walls were given a new underpinning of concrete, and the interior was provided with new foundations, a two-story basement, and a steel frame.

President Truman visited the reconstructed White House on March 27, 1952—two days before announcing that he would not seek reelection. The building now had fifty-four rooms instead of the previous forty-eight.

Furnishing of the White House has varied greatly over the years, reflecting shifting tastes in society at large. Even today, each presidential family may decorate the second- and third-floor private quarters as it wishes.

Four rooms of the second-floor family quarters are worth special mention. The Yellow Oval Room, a formal drawing room with eighteenth century French furniture, opens onto the Truman balcony (added in 1948). The view from there of the Washington Monument and the Jefferson Memorial is regarded as one of the city's finest. Next door to the Yellow Oval Room on the east is the Treaty Room, which was used for cabinet meetings until the Theodore Roosevelt administration. Farther to the east lie the Queen's Bedroom and the Lincoln Bedroom.

Other parts of the family quarters on the second and third floors of the White House were redecorated by President Ronald Reagan and his wife, Nancy, in 1981-1982. They raised nearly $1 million from friends and supporters to have the work done. The net effect was to impart a lighter, more contemporary atmosphere to living spaces that some presidential families have found confining.

As a parting gift, the Reagans had a $49,625 handmade carpet installed in the Oval Office in 1988. But the carpet was not to the liking of George and Barbara Bush, who replaced it in 1990, barely a year after President Bush took office.

But it is difficult even for presidents to change the appearance of the public rooms on the main floor of the White House. These rooms have come to be regarded as almost a museum, especially since Jacqueline Kennedy—the wife of President John F. Kennedy—launched a campaign in the early 1960s to furnish them with authentic items from the late eighteenth and early nineteenth centuries. Any major alterations to the public rooms must now be approved by the Committee for the Preservation of the White House, established by executive order in 1964.

The White House

South Portico

The White House Today

The White House contains 132 rooms, including 32 bathrooms. The residence, which is 170 feet long and 85 feet wide, comprises four floors (referred to as the ground, first, second, and third floors) and two basements; the West and East wings each have three floors. The ground floor, opening onto the South Portico, is visible only from the south side of the house. The five state rooms open for tours are on the first floor, which contains the main, North Portico entrance facing Pennsylvania Avenue. The second floor contains seven historic rooms and the principal living quarters. On the third floor are additional

Executive Branch

rooms for the first family, the solarium, guest bedrooms, and storage areas.

The Committee for the Preservation of the White House works closely with the White House Historical Association, a nonprofit organization, to acquire furniture, paintings, and decorative objects through private donations. At the beginning of each presidential term since 1925, Congress has appropriated $50,000 for the president to paint and decorate the family living quarters.

East Wing and Ground Floor

The public tour of the White House begins in the *East Wing Lobby,* a wood-paneled hall decorated with portraits of first ladies. The East Wing, built in 1902 during Theodore Roosevelt's administration, was rebuilt and enlarged in 1934 by Franklin D. Roosevelt. It contains the visitors' office and the offices of the first lady's staff, the president's military aides, the White House congressional liaison staff, and the Uniformed Division of the Secret Service. In 1942 Roosevelt added the East Wing Lobby and converted the cloakroom—known as the "Hat Box"—into a movie theater, still in use today.

Adjacent to the lobby is the bright, informal *Garden Room,* which overlooks the Jacqueline Kennedy Garden. Visitors proceed through a glass-enclosed colonnade, built on the foundations of Thomas Jefferson's east pavilion, to the ground floor of the White House. Before the renovation of 1902, the *Ground Floor Corridor* (the only area open to the public on this floor) and adjacent rooms served as work and storage areas. The Truman renovation restored the clean lines of Hoban's groined arches and covered the walls and floors with marble. Portaits of first ladies hang in the hall.

The first room on the south side of the corridor is the *Vermeil Room* (also called the "Gold Room"), which contains a collection of gilded silver, given to the White House in 1956 by Margaret Thompson Biddle. Hanging on the south wall is Douglas Chandor's 1949 portrait of Eleanor Roosevelt, who, not liking to sit for portraits, wrote in one corner of the canvas, "A trial made pleasant by the painter." Above the fireplace on the west wall is Claude Monet's "Morning on the Seine," the painting the Kennedy family gave to the White House in 1963 in memory of President Kennedy. This display room also is used as a women's sitting room on formal occasions; a powder room is adjacent.

The second room on the south side of the corridor is the *China Room,* so named in 1917 by Edith Bolling Wilson,

The White House

East Room after Grant administration redecoration

Woodrow Wilson's second wife, to display the china collection begun by Caroline Harrison in 1889. Almost every presidential administration is represented. The white, red, and gold state china service commissioned by Nancy Reagan was donated to the White House in 1982. Howard Chandler Christy's 1924 portrait of Grace Coolidge wearing a red dress determined the red and white color scheme of this room.

Portraits of the most recent first ladies hang on either side of the door to the *Diplomatic Reception Room.* Opening onto the South Portico, the Diplomatic Reception Room contains the south entrance to the White House, used by the first family and foreign dignitaries on informal occasions. (For state dinners, heads of state enter through the North Portico on the first floor; all other guests pass through security checks in the East Wing.) Franklin Roosevelt broadcast his fireside chats from this room in the 1930s and 1940s. In 1961 Jacqueline Kennedy redecorated the room with historic furnishings. "Scenic America," a wallpaper printed in 1834, forms a panorama of American scenes along the curved walls, one of Hoban's three oval rooms.

Executive Branch

For President Roosevelt during World War II, the *Map Room,* next door to the Diplomatic Reception Room, served as a communications center where he tracked the movement of troops and ships. Today, the president and first lady use the room for private meetings and small receptions.

On the north side of the Ground Floor corridor is the *Library.* Used for storage in 1801, later as a laundry room, and in Theodore Roosevelt's day as a "Gentlemen's ante-room," the Library assumed its present use in 1937. Old timbers removed from the house during the Truman restoration were made into wood paneling for the room, now painted a soft grey after the fashion of "painted" rooms in the early 1800s. On the west wall are the original architectural drawings James Hoban and Thomas Jefferson submitted in the 1792 competition for White House architect. In 1961 a committee was formed to select books on American subjects for the Library. The collection for the Library and for the family living quarters continues to grow with presidential biographies and papers and with quadrennial gifts of almost three hundred titles from the American Booksellers Association.

Also on the ground floor are the main kitchen, the florist's workshop, and offices of the curator, the housekeeper, the president's physician, and the auditor.

First Floor

The rooms on the first, or state, floor are those viewed by the public on morning tours and used by the president for official entertaining at other times. The five state rooms—the East Room, Green Room, Blue Room, Red Room, and State Dining Room—are the most historic and the most used parts of the White House. Consequently, they undergo the most refurbishing.

The *North Entrance Hall,* opening onto the North Portico, and the *Cross Hall,* connecting the East Room and the State Dining Room, were part of Hoban's original design. The only major change since Hoban's time took place in 1902 when the main staircase at the west end of the Cross Hall was removed and a new one was installed across from the Green Room. During the Truman restoration, the staircase was repositioned so that it now descends into the Entrance Hall. Also between 1949 and 1952, marble was added to the floors and walls of the Cross Hall, where portraits of recent presidents hang.

The elegant but sparsely furnished *East Room* is probably the most famous room in the White House, for it is here that

The White House

most White House press conferences are held. Decorated in the classical style of the late eighteenth century, the East Room appears today much as it did after the 1902 renovation by the architectural firm McKim, Mead, and White. It is eighty feet long by forty feet wide, with ceilings twenty-two feet in height. The walls are paneled in wood, intricately carved, and painted white. Three Bohemian cut-glass chandeliers hang above an oak floor of Fontainebleu parquetry. The principal article of furniture is a Steinway grand piano with gilded legs in the shape of American eagles, which the Steinway Company donated to the White House in 1938. On the wall is the full-length Gilbert Stuart portrait of George Washington that Dolley Madison saved from the fire of 1814.

In addition to news conferences, the East Room is used for large gatherings on many sorts of occasions—bill signings, receptions, dances, concerts, after-dinner entertainment, weddings, and funerals. It was here that Abigail Adams hung her laundry in 1801; James Madison met with his cabinet in 1812; and Abraham Lincoln dreamed he saw his catafalque surrounded by mourners in 1865—which, but a few days later, it

East Room after Theodore Roosevelt renovation, largely as it appears today

Executive Branch

was. President Grover Cleveland married Frances Folsom in the East Room in 1886 (the only White House wedding of a president); Theodore Roosevelt's children roller skated in the early 1900s; and cellist Pablo Casals performed for Kennedy guests in 1961. Seven presidents have lain in state in the East Room: W. H. Harrison in 1841, Lincoln in 1865, Garfield in 1881, McKinley in 1901, Warren G. Harding in 1923, Franklin Roosevelt in 1945, and Kennedy in 1963.

On the tour, visitors enter the East Room from the Cross Hall and exit through a door to the *Green Room*. Hoban called this room the "Common Dining Room," but only Thomas Jefferson used it regularly for meals. For James Madison, it was a sitting room; for James Monroe, a card room. John Quincy Adams called it the "Green Drawing Room," establishing both its color and its function for future presidents. In the Green Room today small receptions and teas are held and occasionally a small formal dinner.

The room is furnished with Sheraton pieces from the Federal period (1800-1815), many from the New York workshop of cabinetmaker Duncan Phyfe. The walls are covered in green watered-silk, a fabric originally chosen by Jacqueline Kennedy in 1961 and matched and replaced by Patricia Nixon in 1971. The carpet in the Green Room, a large, multicolored Turkish Hereke, is unusual for its green field. On the walls are portraits of presidents and other paintings by well-known American artists.

Hoban designed three oval rooms for the White House, one on each floor at the midpoint of the south side of the house. The *Blue Room,* which Hoban called the "elliptic saloon," is the most historic of the three. Thomas Jefferson first decorated the room in blue, which for most of its history has been used for formal receptions. (The Blue Room also is where the White House Christmas tree is put up each year.) After the fire of 1814, President Monroe decorated the room with French Empire furnishings, largely with pieces made by Pierre Antoine Bellangé. Items from Monroe's collection that were lost or sold at auction in the nineteenth century gradually have been located or reproduced in the twentieth. Refurbishings of 1902, 1962, and 1972 have fully restored the French Empire style of the room.

The fourth state room open to the public, and the third of the three parlors on the first floor, is the *Red Room*. Decorated in the American Empire style (1810-1830) with red damask upholstery and wallpaper of red twill satin, the room has been used as a parlor since Jefferson's day. Earlier, it was John

The White House

Adams's breakfast room. Dolley Madison held her glittering Wednesday night receptions here, and Eleanor Roosevelt held press conferences in this room for women reporters, who were not allowed to attend her husband's meetings with the press. The Red Room gained political fame in 1877 as the place where Rutherford B. Hayes secretly was sworn into office during a party hosted by retiring president Ulysses S. Grant. Because of a close race and a final decision challenged by Hayes's opponent, Grant was eager to ensure a smooth transition of government.

The last of the five state rooms on the public tour is the *State Dining Room*. First given this name by Andrew Jackson, the room earlier served as a drawing room, cabinet room, and office. The 1902 renovation enlarged the room by extending the north wall and removing the grand stairway at the end of the Cross Hall. The State Dining Room today can seat 140.

Similar to the spacious white and gold East Room, the State Dining Room has wood paneling painted in several shades of antique ivory to highlight the delicately carved Corinthian pilasters and neoclassical frieze. Golden silk damask draperies frame the floor-to-ceiling windows. The mantel over the fireplace is a 1962 reproduction of the bison-head mantel from Theodore Roosevelt's administration. In 1952 Truman replaced the Roosevelt mantel with a simpler molding and declared the original "surplus"; the original mantel today is in the Truman presidential library. The face of the mantel is inscribed with the following passage from a letter John Adams wrote to his wife on his second night in the White House:

I Pray to Heaven to Bestow
the Best of Blessings on
THIS HOUSE
and on All that shall hereafter
Inhabit it. May none but Honest
and Wise Men ever rule under this Roof.

Adjacent to the State Dining Room, in the northwest corner of the first floor, is the smaller *Family Dining Room*. Although President Monroe gave his state dinners here and called it the "Public Dining Room," the room usually has served as the formal dining room for the president's family or for official entertaining of a small number of guests. During formal dinners in the State Dining Room, the staff drape the furniture and use this room as a pantry to lessen the inconvenience of having the kitchen and dining room on separate floors. The Family Dining Room appears today much as it did after the 1902 renovation, when its white vaulted ceiling and

Executive Branch

classical frieze were installed. The walls are painted a light yellow, and the furniture is from the Federal period.

Second and Third Floors

The east half of the second floor contains historic areas—the Queen's Suite, the Lincoln Suite, the Treaty Room, and the Yellow Oval Room. The west half contains several rooms of the family living quarters. The third floor comprises additional family rooms as well as sitting rooms and bedrooms for guests. None of these rooms is open to the public, but that has not always been so.

Historic Areas. "All sorts of people come upon all sorts of errands," wrote an assistant to Abraham Lincoln about the crowds milling about in the second-floor hall near the president's office. Throughout the nineteenth century, before offices were moved to the West Wing, the public was free to come and go—and wait—in what is now the *East Sitting Hall.* The room today is a small parlor, furnished largely with antiques from the White House collection, including a seventeenth-century armchair used by George Washington in his rented presidential residence in Philadelphia. Filling the east wall of the hall, overlooking the East Wing and the Treasury Building, is Hoban's original double-arched window.

To the north of the East Sitting Room is the *Queens' Suite,* comprising a small sitting room and a bedroom furnished in the American Federal style. The bed in the *Queens' Bedroom* is believed to have belonged to Andrew Jackson. The *Queens' Sitting Room* appears today much as it did during the Kennedy administration. Wallcovering, draperies, and upholstery are made from a French fabric with ivory, neoclassical medallions on a blue field. The room is furnished with antiques from the American and French Empire periods held in the White House collection. Among the guests who have occupied the Queens' Suite are Queen Elizabeth, wife of Great Britain's King George VI, and her daughter Queen Elizabeth II; and Queen Wilhelmina of the Netherlands and Queen Juliana, her daughter.

On the south side of the East Sitting Hall is the *Lincoln Suite,* comprising the *Lincoln Bedroom* and the *Lincoln Sitting Room.* Used today as a guest room for friends of the president, the bedroom once was Lincoln's office and cabinet room. It was there that he signed the Emancipation Proclamation on January 1, 1863.

President Truman decorated the room with American Victorian furnishings from the period 1850-1870. Notable are

The White House

What's in a Name?

Along the East Coast of the United States, guides at historic sites often claim that "George Washington slept here." Although there is much uncertainty about just where the nation's first president did lodge, historians are sure about one thing—Washington never spent a night in the White House. In fact, Washington is the only president who never lived in the building known around the world as the symbol of the U.S. presidency.

French engineer and architect Pierre Charles L'Enfant, chosen by Washington to plan the capital city, insisted on calling the presidential residence the "President's Palace." But Washington preferred a less regal term and called the residence simply the "President's House." Others spoke of it as the "Executive Mansion."

Once the house was completed its appearance determined its name, for the painted white sandstone stood in sharp contrast to the brick and frame buildings surrounding it. In November 1810 a reporter for the *Baltimore Whig* first referred to the house in print as the "white house." By the end of the James Madison administration in 1817, the term had gained full currency.

Not until 1901, however, did the name become official. In that year Theodore Roosevelt issued an executive order changing the official name from the "Executive Mansion" to the "White House." Today, the president's letterhead reads simply:

The White House
Washington

a desk that Lincoln used and a rosewood bed—eight feet long and six feet wide—thought to have been purchased by Mary Todd Lincoln in 1861. Although Lincoln probably never used the bed, other presidents did, including Theodore Roosevelt and Woodrow Wilson. It is known that Lincoln was particularly fond of the portrait of Andrew Jackson that hangs in the room.

The Lincoln Sitting Room is a small room with a fireplace on the southeast corner of the second floor. Throughout much of the nineteenth century it served as office space for presidential assistants, although English novelist Charles Dickens re-

Executive Branch

corded on his visit to the White House during John Tyler's administration (1841-1845) that this room was the president's office. The Reagans decorated the sitting room with red carpet and upholstery and a patterned wallpaper that complement the Victorian furnishings of the Lincoln Bedroom. The room contains four rosewood chairs purchased by Mrs. Lincoln and a small mahogany desk built by White House architect James Hoban.

Also on the south side of the building, beside the Lincoln Bedroom, is the *Treaty Room,* so named during the Kennedy administration. The Treaty Room served as the cabinet room from 1865 to 1902 and as a sitting room from 1902 to 1961. Since 1961 presidents have signed several important documents here, including U.S. instruments of ratification for the 1963 test ban treaty and the 1972 antiballistic missile treaty.

The furnishings in this room mirror the style popular during the Grant administration. The maroon draperies and dark green wallpaper are copies of Victorian patterns. In 1869 President Grant purchased the large Victorian walnut table in the center of the room, which contains locking drawers for each of his eight cabinet members. On March 26, 1979, President Jimmy Carter had this table moved outdoors for the signing of the Egyptian-Israeli peace treaty.

Adjacent to the Treaty Room is the *Yellow Oval Room,* the third in the tier of Hoban's elliptical rooms. Today the room serves as a formal drawing room for the first family and as a reception room where the president greets foreign dignitaries before state luncheons and dinners. Throughout its history, the room has seen many other uses as well. President John Adams held the first White House reception here on January 1, 1801. It has been a bedroom, a family room, and an office, and Abigail Fillmore set up the first White House library here. Franklin Roosevelt and Harry Truman called the room their "oval study" and used it as a less formal working space than the Oval Office.

Dolley Madison decorated the room in yellow damask in 1809, and Jacqueline Kennedy chose a yellow color scheme again in 1961 when she added furnishings in the neoclassical style of Louis XVI. The Yellow Oval Room contains the works of several important American artists, such as William Merritt Chase and Albert Bierstadt.

The Yellow Oval Room opens onto the Truman balcony, built in 1948, where first families occasionally dine, entertain guests, and on July 4 watch fireworks on the Mall.

The yellow and white *Center Hall* is today a large drawing

The White House

room for the president's family and for foreign guests waiting to be received in the Yellow Oval Room. During the Truman administration, a cornice and bookshelves were installed. The hall is furnished with late eighteenth- and early nineteenth-century antiques from the White House collection and, like the Yellow Oval Room, is decorated with works of American artists.

Family Living Quarters. With each first family, both the decor and the number of rooms used as the family living quarters change, for they become the Washington home of the person elected president. These rooms constitute a private home within a very public house; comfort and familiarity, not the historical record, govern their use and appearance.

This part of the White House has been changing constantly, as President Truman discovered when he asked Chief Usher J. B. West whether his family's plan for the living quarters would be "tampering with history too much." West replied:

> The President may use the house any way he wishes.... It's always been so. Actually, the room that Mrs. Truman has chosen for her sitting room was probably where Lincoln slept. The Coolidges kept the Lincoln furniture there, and President and Mrs. Coolidge slept in the room together. The Hoovers slept in the same room, but they moved the Lincoln furniture across the hall.... You could just as easily move it down the hall over the East Room, because that was the Lincoln Cabinet Room.

To this convoluted history lesson Truman replied, "Now I know why they say Lincoln's ghost walks around up here all night. He's just looking for his bed!"

The West Sitting Hall, opening off the Center Hall, is the first family's private living room, which, with each new administration, is decorated with personal items from the family's former home. Like the East Sitting Hall, one end of the room is dominated by Hoban's double-arched window, which overlooks the West Wing and the Old Executive Office Building. Before the 1902 renovation, this hall was little more than a stair landing. During the Truman renovation, the hall became a room when it was enclosed with solid partitions.

Jacqueline Kennedy disliked the Family Dining Room on the first floor and wanted a smaller, more intimate dining room for her family in their living quarters. So in 1961 she converted one of the Eisenhowers' sitting rooms on the north side of the West Sitting Hall into the President's Dining Room. Early in the century, this space had served as a bedroom, and Alice

Executive Branch

Roosevelt Longworth, daughter of Theodore Roosevelt, remembered having her appendix removed here.

The President's Dining Room is furnished largely with American Federal pieces donated to the White House in 1961 and 1962 through Jacqueline Kennedy's Fine Arts Committee. The mahogany sideboard was once owned by Daniel Webster; it still bears his initials. James Madison's portable, walnut medicine chest on display here was taken from the house by a British soldier just before troops burned the mansion in 1814. A Canadian descendant of the soldier donated the chest to the White House in 1939. The wallpaper, called "The War of Independence," is a panorama of scenes from the American Revolution—some accurate in their details, some merely imagined by the artist.

The first family's private kitchen, also built in 1961, is adjacent to the dining room on the northwest corner of the second floor. This was not, however, the first private kitchen in the family living quarters. Franklin Roosevelt did not like the food his wife's cook prepared, so in 1938 he had a kitchen built on the third floor and brought in his own cook from his Hyde Park home. Thereafter he took many of his meals with friends or staff in his second-floor study (now the Yellow Oval Room).

Like many presidents before him, President Reagan used a private, second-floor study in addition to the West Wing Oval Office. This room, adjoining the Yellow Oval Room on the south side of the house, had been the bedroom of presidents Franklin Roosevelt through Nixon. President Ford used this room as a sitting room, as did President Carter, who had a wall of mahogany bookcases built. On the side of the mantelpiece is a small plaque that Jacqueline Kennedy had installed after her husband's assassination; it reads: "This room was occupied by John Fitzgerald Kennedy during the two years, ten months and two days he was President of the United States. January 20, 1961-November 22, 1963."

President and Mrs. Bush shared the bedroom adjacent to the president's study, as did the Fords, the Carters, and the Reagans. In earlier administrations, Mamie Eisenhower, Jacqueline Kennedy, Lady Bird Johnson, and Patricia Nixon made this room their bedroom. First families since the Eisenhowers have used the small adjoining room in the southwest corner of the second floor as a dressing room.

A small room just above the North Portico entrance served as Nancy Reagan's private study. She converted another room in the living quarters into an exercise room.

Family quarters extend to the third floor, although not all

South Portico, Truman balcony on second floor

first families have used these rooms regularly. The Third Floor Center Sitting Hall, lined with bookshelves, follows the decorating style of the Central Hall on the second floor. Various parlors and guest bedrooms open onto the hall. The Solarium—or "sky parlor," as Grace Coolidge called it—has been a favorite retreat of first families since 1927. It served, for example, as a schoolroom for Caroline Kennedy, an entertaining room for Luci and Lynda Johnson (who had a soda fountain installed there), and a family room for the Carters. Octag-

Executive Branch

onal in shape with three walls of glass, the room overlooks the south lawn of the White House and the Mall. Outside the Solarium, hidden behind the balustrade, is a space large enough for sunbathing.

West Wing

The West Wing of the White House is where the chief executive conducts the official business of the presidency. Built during the Roosevelt renovation of 1902 as temporary offices, the wing has since become a permanent addition to the White House. It was doubled in size in 1909 and enlarged again in 1927 and 1934. The structure was rebuilt in 1930 after a fire on Christmas Eve, 1929.

In 1969 President Nixon remodeled the West Wing. A north portico and driveway were added to the front of the building, and the swimming pool along the colonnade joining the West Wing and the mansion was boarded over to make more room for the press. The old press lobby, in use since 1902 on the north side of the wing, was converted to the *West Wing Reception Room* and is used today as an appointments lobby.

High-level staff meetings and conferences are held in the *Roosevelt Room,* which President Nixon named for both Theodore and Franklin Roosevelt, in honor of their contributions to the construction and expansion of the West Wing. Service flags from the United States Army, Navy, Air Force, Marine Corps, and Coast Guard stand at one end of the large conference table, which dominates the room. On one wall is the medal presented to Theodore Roosevelt in 1906 when he won the Nobel Peace Prize for his role in settling the Russo-Japanese War. Today the room is decorated with presidential portraits and American landscape paintings, but during Franklin Roosevelt's administration it looked quite different. The New Deal president installed an aquarium and filled the room with mementoes of his fishing trips, so the staff called it the "Fish Room." The tradition continued through the Kennedy administration when the president mounted a sailfish on the wall.

In the *Cabinet Room,* added to the West Wing in 1909, the president meets with the cabinet, the National Security Council, and members of Congress and occasionally conducts award ceremonies. An oval, mahogany conference table seating twenty, purchased by President Nixon in 1970, fills the room. The president's chair is two inches taller than the others. Overlooking the Rose Garden, the Cabinet Room contains likenesses of former presidents and statesmen—the choice reflecting the preferences of the current chief executive. Presi-

The White House

dent Reagan selected busts of Washington and Benjamin Franklin and portraits of Jefferson, Lincoln, Taft, Coolidge, and Eisenhower.

The *Oval Office* is the president's formal office, where meetings with heads of government and chiefs of state are held. The first Oval Office was built in 1909 in the center of the West Wing; in 1934 it was moved to its current location on the southeast corner of the wing, overlooking the Rose Garden. Each president has decorated the Oval Office to suit his tastes. The only features that remain constant are the presidential seal in the ceiling medallion and the two flags behind the president's desk—the U.S. flag and the president's flag.

For their Oval Office desk, Presidents Reagan and Bush used the one Queen Victoria gave to President Hayes in 1880, made from timbers of the H.M.S. *Resolute*. In 1855 American whalers had rescued the ship trapped in Arctic ice, and the United States returned it to the British government. Later, when the *Resolute* was broken up, Queen Victoria had the desk made for the U.S. president in a gesture of appreciation. Truman used the desk, as did Franklin Roosevelt, who installed a front panel to conceal his leg braces. Kennedy also used the *Resolute* desk, but it was John F. Kennedy, Jr., who made the desk famous in a photograph that was taken of the boy peeking out from behind the central panel while his father worked above.

White House Grounds

The eighteen acres surrounding the White House have changed a great deal since John and Abigail Adams's time. In November 1800 the grounds were muddy and littered with the shacks and supplies of workers still building the mansion.

Methods of groundskeeping have changed as well. The grass, for example, is no longer kept short by grazing sheep, as it was as recently as Woodrow Wilson's administration, or by William Howard Taft's cow, Pauline Wayne. Today, the National Park Service takes care of the house and grounds. Still, touches of the past remain.

Thomas Jefferson was an avid gardener and landscaped what he called the "President's Park." John Quincy Adams devoted much time to the gardens, and a massive American elm that he planted on the south lawn stands today as a monument to his efforts. Growing tall beside the South Portico, the southern magnolias that Andrew Jackson planted in memory of his wife nearly conceal the windows of the president's bedroom on the second floor. Since the Wilson administration, every president has planted trees on the White House grounds.

Executive Branch

Twice a year, in the spring and fall, the grounds are open for public tour.

Special Gardens

The *Rose Garden* is one of three special gardens on the grounds of the White House. Situated between the West Wing and the residence, the Rose Garden is planted in the style of a traditional eighteenth-century American garden. From early spring until the first frost, flowers and trees provide seasonal color within the rectangular frame of boxwood and osmanthus hedges.

Until 1902 conservatories and greenhouses covered the ground where the West Wing and Rose Garden now are. Theodore Roosevelt had them removed. Ellen Axson Wilson first planted roses there in 1913, and the garden remained largely unchanged until 1962 when President Kennedy asked Rachel Lambert Mellon to redesign it.

The president receives special guests in the Rose Garden, such as foreign dignitaries, Medal of Honor winners, and U.S. astronauts. The president sometimes will host a state dinner in the garden. In June 1971 the first outdoor White House wedding took place there, when Tricia Nixon married Edward Cox.

The *Jacqueline Kennedy Garden* is to the first lady what the Rose Garden is to the president. Located beside the East Wing of the White House, the garden is a setting for the first lady's informal receptions. Shaded by rows of lindens, the garden contains ornamental flowering trees and shrubs around a rectangular lawn. Lady Bird Johnson named the garden for her predecessor in 1965, but Patricia Nixon called it "the east garden." Today, it again bears Mrs. Kennedy's name.

On January 18, 1969, Lady Bird Johnson established a third special garden, this one in honor of the young children associated with the White House. Plaques bearing the handprints and footprints of the Johnson grandchildren and two Carter grandchildren decorate the garden.

Recreational Facilities

Presidents through the years have set up their own sports facilities on the White House grounds. Hayes played croquet, Harding played medicine ball, Hoover played golf (and trained his Airedale to retrieve the balls), and Truman played horseshoes. Ford installed the first outdoor swimming pool, and presidents since Theodore Roosevelt have enjoyed the tennis court on the south lawn.

Children, too, have had their fun outdoors at the White

House. Benjamin Harrison's grandson, Baby McKee, rode around the grounds in a cart pulled by His Whiskers—the boy's pet goat. Eleanor Roosevelt had a jungle gym and a sandbox built for her grandchildren and resisted the advice of groundskeepers against hanging an old-fashioned swing from a tree limb. Theodore Roosevelt's son Quentin rode his pony Algonquin on the south lawn, and Caroline Kennedy riding Macaroni was a favorite subject for photographers in the early 1960s.

An annual public treat for children begun in 1879 is the Easter Monday egg-rolling. Children are invited to bring their eggs to the party and compare their artistic and egg-rolling skills. In 1986, thirty-five thousand people attended the event.

Security and Communications

The Secret Service is tight-lipped about White House security procedures, reasoning that the more that is known about its practices the better equipped a potential assassin could be. Yet the Secret Service is keenly aware that the White House is a national monument and an important symbol to the American people. Consequently, the White House—even on a tour of its interior—appears remarkably accessible. It is not.

Round-the-clock protection of the president and the mansion is the duty of plainclothes Secret Service agents (the ones dressed in business suits with small white lapel pins) and of the White House Branch of the Uniformed Division of the Secret Service. The agents, working in eight-hour shifts, are stationed throughout the residence and in the East and West wings. Officers of the Uniformed Division are positioned on the grounds of the residence, at the guardhouses, and at selected posts inside, such as the hallways and entrances to the Oval Office. Two main duties of the Uniformed Division are to police the grounds of the White House and to conduct and monitor visitors' tours.

The White House is surrounded by a black iron fence six and one-half feet tall. Two uniformed guards usually staff each of the small white guardhouses along the perimeter of the grounds, one standing outside, the other watching over surveillance devices inside. Entrance gates to the White House were reinforced in the late 1970s after two gate-crashing incidents.

Electronic sensors and video equipment ensure thorough protection of the grounds. Buried seismic sensors can detect even the lightest footsteps. Television cameras disguised as lanterns or concealed in plantings provide visual surveillance. Uniformed guards regularly check the grounds from observa-

Executive Branch

tion points on the roof of the White House and the Treasury Building next door. Foot and vehicular patrols (on small motorcycles) cover the grounds and the streets around the White House. A canine unit, trained in attacking and scouting, is used primarily to check the buildings and grounds for explosives.

In 1983 security of the house and grounds was stepped up significantly, prompted by several incidents: a bombing at the U.S. Capitol, the receipt of intelligence reports about possible terrorist attacks on the White House, and bombings of the U.S. embassy and the marine barracks in Lebanon. At a cost of $6.9 million, East Executive Avenue was closed and made into a park. A wall of concrete barriers, installed in 1983, was replaced in 1988 by 274 barrel-shaped cement posts linked by heavy chains; they cost $670,000. The posts, thirty-eight inches high and four feet apart, are placed so that only slow-moving vehicles can approach and enter the White House gate.

The Secret Service also must guard the airspace above the White House. It uses monitoring systems to identify aircraft approaching nearby National Airport and shoulder-fired Redeye antiaircraft missiles as a last resort should a plane refuse warnings and approach the President's House. One such incident occurred during the Nixon administration when a discontented twenty-year-old soldier buzzed the White House in a stolen helicopter. Gunfire forced the chopper to land, and the soldier was arrested. He explained that he had not intended to harm the president but "was just kissing off. I wanted to buzz everything that was popular." Further steps to secure White House airspace were taken in 1983 with the installation of fixed-base ground-to-air missiles.

The Uniformed Division also carefully monitors White House tours. Visitors enter through the East Wing and, as at airports, pass through a magnetometer, which checks for concealed metal. Still more sensitive are the devices for detecting radioactive materials. In 1986 two women on a White House tour were questioned by the Secret Service when they set off these alarms. Several days before their White House visit, each had had a radioisotope scan for heart disease, and small amounts of radioactivity remained in their bodies.

The uniformed guards inspect all handbags and packages and ask visitors to leave behind all newspapers, which conceivably could hide a weapon. Guards watch the tourists on closed-circuit television as they make their way through the five rooms and two hallways that are open to the public. Plainclothes Secret Service agents mingle with the visitors, watching and listening for signs of threatening behavior.

The White House

North Portico

Careful security procedures extend well beyond the monitoring of tourists. Electronic sensing devices, embedded in the floors, ceilings, and walls, track all movement in the house. Secret Service agents know at all times exactly where the president is within the White House so that they can maintain a "protective ring" around the chief executive. All visitors and aides, even the president's closest advisers, must wear a visible security badge. Transparent bullet-proof shields cover the windows in the Oval Office, even though the office is not visible from the street. The president has the added security of a knee-high "panic button" located beneath the Oval Office desk. The president can push the button while appearing simply to shift position. Occasionally, the chief executive pushes the button by accident and is startled when a cadre of arms-wielding agents bursts into the office.

The Secret Service inspects all incoming packages and takes no chances with gifts of food—none ever reaches the president. The White House also is equipped with highly sensitive air and water filtration systems for detecting poisonous gas and bacteria. To ensure that no one tampers with the president's food, all food suppliers for the White House are cleared by the Secret Service. Even so, White House kitchen staff hand

Executive Branch

select many food items at random.

One of the most secure—and seldom discussed—areas of the White House is the Situation Room, the presidential communications nerve center. Located under the Oval Office in the basement of the West Wing, the Situation Room is run by a twenty-five-person duty staff of communications experts from the U.S. Army Signal Corps. Twenty-four hours a day they operate the Signal Board, which links the White House with the Pentagon, the State Department, the Central Intelligence Agency, and other military and intelligence facilities. The Situation Room receives some three thousand messages daily. Contrary to popular assumptions, the Washington-Moscow "hot line" is not in the White House; rather, it is part of the National Military Command Center at the Pentagon.

For the president and members of the first family, the White House telephone system provides immediate connections with virtually any place in the world. Without dialing or looking up numbers, they have only to pick up the telephone and tell switchboard operators who and where they want to call.

Whether traveling by plane, car, or ship, walking at Camp David, attending a concert at the Kennedy Center, or visiting a foreign head of state, the president is said to be never more than thirty seconds away from the communications link to the White House command post.

Executive Office Buildings

The Old Executive Office Building (OEOB), formerly the State, War, and Navy Building, may be the government's most maligned structure. Mark Twain called it "the ugliest building in America." Utah senator Reed Smoot said it was "covered with gimcracks and spizzerinktums." Herbert Hoover declared that it was "an architectural absurdity," and Harry Truman described it as "the greatest monstrosity in America." Excessive or engaging, the French Second Empire structure, now a historic landmark, remains a monument to the architectural enthusiasm of a victorious government after the Civil War.

Supervising Architect of the Treasury Alfred Bult Mullett designed the building, constructed from 1871 to 1888, for the State, War, and Navy departments. The State Department's south wing was completed in 1875; the Navy's east wing in 1879; and the War Department's north, west, and center wings in 1888. But these departments continued to grow, and by 1947 each had vacated the building for larger quarters. In 1939 the White House began moving some of its offices into the building, and in 1949 the State, War, and Navy Building was given over entirely to the Executive Office of the President (EOP). Today the building at Pennsylvania Avenue and Seventeenth Street, NW, houses the White House Office, the National Security Council, the Office of Management and Budget, the Council of Economic Advisers, and the vice president's office.

The OEOB comprises 440,250 square feet—including 553 rooms, two miles of black-and-white-tiled corridors, and ten acres of floor space. When completed the OEOB was the largest office building in Washington and among the largest in the world. It is still one of the largest granite buildings, with four-and-one-half-foot exterior walls and many eighteen-foot ceilings. Construction costs totaled $10.1 million.

The French Second Empire styling makes the OEOB architecturally unique in Washington. Some say its seven floors with tier upon tier of columns (some nine hundred in all) look like a wedding cake. Its elaborate dormer windows, mansard roof of light green copper, and more than two dozen chimneys topped with oversize chimney pots make it a curious compan-

Executive Branch

Old Executive Office Building

ion to the Georgian-style White House next door.

In 1934 and 1944 Congress approved plans to give the OEOB a Greek Revival façade to match its neighbor to the east of the White House, the Treasury Building. In 1957 a commission appointed by President Eisenhower recommended its demolition. But funds ran short after each proposal, and the OEOB remained untouched. Although John F. Kennedy's Commission on Fine Arts recommended preservation of the building, full-scale restoration did not get under way until 1981, under President Ronald Reagan's Office of Administration.

When the carpeting, partitions, and dropped ceilings were removed, the three-story White House Law Library, formerly the War Department Library, revealed its colorful Minton tile floor and the delicate cast-iron tracery of its balcony railings. Also restored was the four-story State Department Library, which now serves as the White House Library and Research Center. Both libraries were constructed entirely of cast iron to reduce the danger of fire. The Indian Treaty Room, with its tile floor and coffered ceiling, is used for receptions and award ceremonies.

Executive Office Buildings

> **Visitors Information**
>
> Tours of the Old Executive Office Building take place Saturday mornings, beginning at 9:00 a.m., leaving every twenty minutes; the last one departs at 11:40 a.m. Tours are guided and last one hour.
>
> Reservations are required and may be made by calling (202) 395-5895 from 9:00 a.m. to noon at least as early as the Wednesday before the Saturday you plan to take the tour. Provide your name, date of birth, and social security number. If you are not a U.S. citizen, name and date of birth are sufficient. Each tour accommodates approximately twenty-five to thirty visitors. Group tours are available upon request. Bring positive identification, such as a driver's license, on the day of your tour.
>
> Photography is not permitted inside the building.

Five presidents worked in the OEOB before becoming chief executive, and more than one thousand treaties have been signed within its walls. It was in this building on December 7, 1941, that Secretary of State Cordell Hull confronted the two Japanese envoys who pretended to negotiate peace in the Pacific as Japanese warplanes bombed Pearl Harbor.

Less than twenty-five years after moving into the OEOB, the Executive Office of the President again needed more space. The solution became known as the New Executive Office Building, a ten-story structure completed in 1968, one block from the OEOB at Seventeenth and H streets, NW. Designed by John Carl Warnecke, the contemporary red-brick building contains 307,000 square feet of office space and approximately nine hundred EOP employees.

The Vice President's Residence

On the grounds of the Naval Observatory on Massachusetts Avenue, NW, barely visible from the road, stands the official home of the vice president. Although the president has had an official Washington residence since 1800, not until July 1974 did Congress give the vice president a permanent home. Costs of securing and protecting the house of each new vice president had become greater than the cost of establishing and maintaining a single residence.

Formerly known as the Admiral's House, the residence served as the home of the superintendent of the Naval Observatory until 1928 and of the chief of naval operations until 1974. Adm. Elmo R. Zumwalt was the last military resident of the house.

Designed by Washington architect Leon E. Dessez and completed in 1893, the white brick Queen Anne-style house comprises a basement and three floors—twelve rooms plus service areas and six bathrooms (four full and two half-baths). On the first floor an entrance hall, dining room, living room, sitting room, and sunroom provide space for entertaining. Because the dining room can accommodate only thirty persons, vice presidents often have entertained large numbers of guests outdoors. A bedroom, sitting room, and bath form the master suite on the second floor, which also contains an office and a guest bedroom. Another bedroom and three smaller rooms (once maids' rooms) are on the third floor. The kitchen, laundry, and quarters for the staff are in the basement. A back staircase runs from the butler's pantry on the first floor to the third story, through a back hall on each floor.

Outside, a pillared porte cochere forms the main entrance. A wide veranda extends from the right of the entrance along the front of the house and curves around the three-story Romanesque tower on the south, forming a porch on three sides. The steep roof of grey slate contains the three dormer windows of the third floor. The house is situated on twelve acres, landscaped in the style of an English park.

When Congress claimed the Admiral's House for the vice president in 1974, it appropriated $315,000 for renovation and installation of security devices. At that time the roof leaked, the floors sagged, the six fireplaces did not work, the wiring was unsafe, and the house was air-conditioned with twenty-two window units (since replaced with central air-conditioning). In the late 1980s the annual appropriation for operating the residence was $258,000, which included $75,000 for entertaining. The navy, which still owns and maintains the house, also supplies staff for the vice president's residence, including six enlistees who serve as stewards.

Although the house has been available to five vice presidents, only three have lived there. Mrs. Gerald R. Ford began plans for decorating but had time to do little more than select china and crystal before her husband became president in August 1974. Vice President and Mrs. Nelson Rockefeller (1974-1977) continued to live in their home on Foxhall Road in Washington, but they supervised the renovation and contributed several pieces of their own artwork and furnishings to the house. One controversial Rockefeller donation was a $35,000 bed by Surrealist artist Max Ernst, titled "Cage Bed with Screen." The bed eventually left the residence, but an Adams-style dining room table that had belonged to the Rockefeller family remains.

Vice President and Mrs. Walter F. Mondale (1977-1981) and their three children were the first full-time residents. Mrs. Mondale, an art historian, used the house as a showcase for works of contemporary American artists. The Mondales also established a household library of works by and about vice presidents.

Vice President and Mrs. George Bush (1981-1989) discovered the limitations of the initial $315,000 appropriation when the roof began to leak again, mortar between bricks began crumbling, and damp streaks appeared on the living room walls. As a result, the navy spent more than $240,000 for repairs. The Bushes redecorated the house through approximately $200,000 in private donations and restored the interior by adding their personal furnishings and paintings borrowed from art museums in Washington and Houston.

Vice President Dan Quayle and his family moved into the mansion in January 1989. Marilyn Quayle soon found the house inadequate for her three young children and personally lobbied Congress for more repair and maintenance money than the $378,000 President Bush had requested. She got her wish: Congress added $200,000 to begin the remodeling and the administration doubled the next year's request for the mansion. The work began in 1990 and was to include new upstairs bedrooms and a bathroom for the children, an office for Mrs. Quayle, and general repairs.

Departmental Headquarters

When the federal government moved from Philadelphia to Washington, D.C., in 1800, the executive branch consisted of four departments—State, Treasury, War, and Navy. By 1820 each had its own brick building within short walking distance of the president's office in the White House. The entire executive branch was neatly contained within two city blocks. Today, there are fourteen departments and more than five hundred executive branch buildings in the Washington, D.C., area.

Only the Treasury Department is located on approximately its original site. Like its neighbors the White House and the Old Executive Office Building, it is a historic landmark, as designated by the interior secretary's National Park System Advisory Board.

Other departmental buildings are unusual for their history, their artwork (the Justice and Interior buildings contain exceptional examples of American art of the 1930s), or, simply, their size. Several were considered to be the largest office building in the world when completed. Today, it is said that the Pentagon holds that distinction.

Several of the older departmental headquarters are located in the so-called Federal Triangle, bounded on the north by Pennsylvania Avenue, on the east by Sixth Street, on the south by Constitution Avenue, and on the west by the Ellipse in front of the White House.

Department of Agriculture

The Department of Agriculture headquarters on Fourteenth Street, SW, is contained in two structures—the Administration Building facing the Mall and the South Building facing Independence Avenue. The two are joined by two third-floor archways over Independence Avenue and an underground tunnel.

The neoclassical Administration Building, designed by Rankin, Kellogg, and Crane of Philadelphia, was built in three sections, largely of marble. The four-story, L-shaped east and west wings, constructed from 1904 to 1908, set the precedent for a four-hundred-foot setback from the center line of the Mall. The five-story center section, with its imposing Corinthian colonnade, connects the east and west wings. It was built

Executive Branch

from 1928 to 1930. The Administration Building contains a gross floor area of 380,000 square feet, with 280,000 square feet of offices and other work areas. The secretary of agriculture's office is in this part of the departmental headquarters.

The seven-story South Building, with nearly six times as much office space as the Administration Building, was designed in the office of the Supervising Architect of the Treasury and constructed from 1930 to 1937. It contains seven miles of corridors and 1.5 million square feet of office space, divided into more than four thousand rooms. Its seven wings and six interior courtyards cover three city blocks. The exterior of the building is neoclassical but less ornamented than the Administration Building. The Twelfth Street and Fourteenth Street wings are finished in limestone; the rest of the exterior, in variegated tan brick and terra-cotta.

Approximately ten thousand people work in the headquarters building, which contains all but two bureaus of the Agriculture Department. Agriculture has field offices in every state and most major cities throughout the United States, including more than seventy Extension Service locations and approximately fifty offices of the Farmers Home Administration.

Department of Commerce

The Herbert Clark Hoover Building, named in 1982 for the former president (1929-1933) and commerce secretary (1921-1928), was the largest office building in the world when completed in 1932. The building encompasses 1.1 million square feet of work space, covers eight acres, contains 3,311 rooms, and houses approximately forty-two hundred employees.

Construction of the seven-story building, designed by the New York architectural firm of York and Sawyer, began in 1927 on swampland the government purchased in 1910 for $2.5 million. The Commerce building sits atop Tiber Creek, and sections of the basement floor are three feet thick to withstand pressure from the water flowing underneath.

The building comprises three large rectangular sections joined by accordion-like expansion joints. Because these joints expand in the heat and contract in the cold, the Hoover Building may be three inches longer in July than it is in January. Filling three city blocks, Commerce forms the western side of the Federal Triangle and is bounded by Fourteenth and Fifteenth streets, NW, on the east and west and by D Street and Constitution Avenue on the north and south. It cost $17.5 million to build.

Two unusual features of the building are on view to the

Departmental Headquarters

> ## Visitors Information
>
> Guided public tours are available of the Pentagon, the State Department diplomatic reception rooms, and the Department of the Treasury.
>
> Tours of the Pentagon, which houses the Department of Defense, are given from 9:30 a.m. to 3:30 p.m., Monday through Friday, except on national holidays. Admission is on a first-come, first-serve basis for individuals and small groups. Reservations, however, are required for a group tour of twenty-five or more. Call (202) 695-1776 at least two weeks in advance. Photography is permitted in hallways and exhibit areas but not inside the offices. Brochures are available in French, German, Spanish, and Japanese.
>
> Sixteen rooms furnished with antiques of the American classical period are on view at the State Department. Guided tours, which require reservations ((202) 647-3241), are available at 9:30 a.m., 10:30 a.m., and 3:00 p.m., Monday through Friday, and last about forty-five minutes. Entrance for the tours is at 2201 C Street, NW.
>
> Tours of the Treasury Department are offered every other Saturday beginning at 10:00 a.m., 10:20 a.m., and 10:40 a.m. Reservations are required. Call (202) 343-9136 and provide your date of birth and social security number for a security clearance. Sign at entrance for tours is marked "Employee Entrance."

public. A census "clock" digitally records births and deaths in the United States, showing an American born every eight seconds and dying every fifteen seconds (for a population growth rate of 0.9 percent). A basement aquarium displays more than one thousand fish from around the world.

Department of Defense

The Pentagon—headquarters of the Department of Defense (DOD)—is located in Arlington, Virginia, just across the Potomac River from Washington, D.C. Said to be the world's largest office building, it is the only departmental headquarters outside the District of Columbia.

Gen. Brehon B. Somervell's 1941 plan to house the nation's military establishment under one roof aroused controversy, but pressures of impending war hastened congressional approval of new headquarters for what later became the De-

Executive Branch

fense Department. The government already owned more than half of the 583 acres needed for the proposed building, and it bought the rest—mostly swamps, dumps, and dilapidated buildings—for $2.2 million. Starting in August 1941, thirteen thousand laborers worked in shifts around the clock and completed construction in January 1943—a mere seventeen months later. The building itself cost $49.6 million; the total project, including outside facilities, $83.0 million.

With a gross floor area of 6.5 million square feet (3.7 million of which is work space), the Pentagon contains three times the floor space of the Empire State Building. Its other statistics also are impressive. The building covers twenty-nine acres and contains 150 stairways, 19 escalators, 13 elevators, 280 restrooms, 7,748 windows, and fifteen thousand light fixtures. The parking lot covers sixty-seven acres and has space for almost ten thousand cars. Twenty-six thousand military and civilian employees use the stores, restaurants, theaters, barbershop, post office, education centers, and libraries within the building. Each day, the Pentagon post office handles 130,000 pieces of mail, while the building's 22,500 telephones accommodate 200,000 calls.

Architects George E. Bergstrom and David J. Whitmer designed the five-sided steel and concrete structure to fit its site, which is bounded by five roads. The number five recurs throughout the building's design. Besides having five sides, the Pentagon contains five concentric rings; that is, the exterior ring surrounds four progressively smaller pentagons, each with five floors. A center courtyard with grass and trees covers five acres.

The total length of Pentagon hallways is seventeen and one-half miles, but because ten spoke-like corridors connect the five rings, it takes no more than seven minutes to walk from any one point to another.

Armed forces guides at the Pentagon take visitors through displays of model ships, art depicting scenes from World War II, and memorials to military heroes. Two such exhibits are the Hall of Heroes, commemorating the four thousand Congressional Medal of Honor winners, and the corridor honoring the twenty-four hundred Americans listed as Prisoners of War/Missing in Action in the Vietnam War.

Also at the Pentagon but not on view to the public is the Washington-Moscow Direct Communications Link, better known as the "hot line." It was set up in 1963 in response to the Cuban missile crisis and is located in the National Military Command Center.

Vast though the Pentagon is, less than 1 percent of the

Departmental Headquarters

Defense Department's 3.2 million employees work there. (Defense employs 1.1 million civilian and 2.1 million military personnel.) Approximately one hundred fifty thousand people work at more than twenty-five other Defense facilities in the Washington area—workplaces as diverse as the Walter Reed Army Medical Center, the Naval Observatory, and the National War College. DOD comprises 871 military installations in the United States and 393 abroad.

Department of Education

The Education headquarters, at 400 Maryland Avenue, SW, is housed in Federal Office Building (FOB) No. 6, one of several modern, numbered office structures commissioned in the late 1950s in southwest Washington to accommodate the growing executive branch bureaucracy. FOB 6, designed by two Washington, D.C., firms—Faulkner, Kingsbury, and Stenhouse; and Chatelain, Gauger, and Holan—was built between 1959 and 1961 at a cost of $13.3 million. Its several hundred tall, narrow windows on the second through the sixth floors give an impression of greater height to the eight-story limestone building.

FOB 6 contains 401,544 square feet of office space and houses fifteen hundred workers; approximately nine hundred work for Education, the remainder for the National Aeronautics and Space Administration. Education staffers work in two other buildings in Washington and in ten regional offices throughout the country.

Executive Branch

Department of Energy

The Department of Energy moved into the James Forrestal Building at 1000 Independence Avenue, SW, in 1977, the year the department was established. For its first seven years the building had housed employees of the Defense Department. In December 1963 Congress appropriated $33.7 million for the structure known as FOB (Federal Office Building) No. 5 until it was named for former secretary of defense Forrestal. The contemporary-styled building of precast concrete was under construction from September 1965 to April 1970 and was designed by the architectural firms of Curtis and Davis, Fordyce and Hanby Associates, Frank Grad and Sons.

The Forrestal Building is a sprawling, three-part structure with 1.1 million square feet of occupiable space in floors above and below ground. The South Building has eight floors above ground; the North Building has four; the West Building, two. Each part is constructed of architectural concrete with recessed window pockets one story tall. The three wings are connected by two floors of office space underground. The Forrestal Building houses forty-five hundred employees and all divisions of the Energy Department, except for the Federal Energy Regulatory Commission offices, which are on Capitol Hill.

Department of Health and Human Services

The Hubert H. Humphrey Building, headquarters of the Department of Health and Human Services (HHS) at 200 Independence Avenue, SW, is one of two departmental headquarters designed by architect Marcel Breuer. Under construction from 1971 to 1975, the contemporary steel and concrete structure is heavily fenestrated with hundreds of convex trapezoidal windows cantilevered over the first floor. The walls of windows break off at each corner, leaving recesses for shafts, discreetly incorporated into the building's design, to vent exhaust fumes from the freeway tunnel that passes underneath.

The twelve-story building houses approximately eighteen hundred HHS staffers in 328,490 square feet of office space. The remaining 22,100 HHS employees in the Washington, D.C., area are scattered among fifty-nine other buildings, including the Parklawn Building in Rockville, Maryland, housing approximately six thousand staffers. HHS employs more than 125,000 people throughout the United States in regional and field offices of the Social Security Administration, the Public Health Service, and other HHS agencies.

Department of Housing and Urban Development

The Housing and Urban Development (HUD) building, at Seventh and D streets, SW, was the first of two departmental headquarters that the federal government commissioned from architect Marcel Breuer. Similar in design to Breuer's UNESCO headquarters in Paris, HUD is unique among Washington buildings for its curvilinear shape: from above, it looks like two *Y*'s joined at their base. The American Institute of Architects awarded Breuer its 1968 gold medal for this design and other work.

Built between 1965 and 1968 at a cost of $22.5 million, HUD was the first federal structure made of precast concrete, a mark of the International style. The sculptural effects of precast concrete are apparent in the 1,585 recessed window units, each weighing ten tons, that form the curve of the walls. The building's ten stories rest on dozens of *pilotis,* or pillars, creating a 5.5-acre courtyard instead of a first floor at ground level.

Unlike the straight, seemingly endless hallways of the Pentagon (875 feet) and other government buildings, the longest corridor at HUD (180 feet) seems even shorter because the curving walls create an optical illusion that gives the building a more human scale. The building contains 543,000 square feet of office space for the forty-two hundred employees working there.

HUD has eighty-one regional and field offices throughout the United States. All of its Washington bureaus are housed within the headquarters building.

Department of the Interior

The Department of the Interior building, at Eighteenth and C streets, NW, three blocks southwest of the White House, was the first project undertaken by the Public Works Administration (PWA) to provide work for the unemployed during the New Deal era. Constructed in only sixteen months, from August 1935 to December 1936, the eight-story granite and limestone building contains sixteen acres of floor space and two miles of corridors, housing twenty-nine hundred employees.

President Franklin D. Roosevelt laid the cornerstone in 1936 with the same trowel George Washington had used to lay the Capitol cornerstone in 1793.

The building, designed by Waddy B. Wood, is utilitarian and plain on the outside but has an elaborately decorated interior containing more New Deal art than any other government structure. Bas-reliefs and murals by Heinz Warneke and Louis Bouché, among others, depict the themes and work of the department. Notable among Interior's murals is Henry Varnum Poor's nine-by-forty-two-foot work showing the origins of the conservation movement in the United States.

Harold Ickes, interior secretary from 1933 to 1946 and

Executive Branch

head of PWA, took a keen interest not only in the building but in a state-of-the-art museum with exhibits of the department's programs. Today, one still can see the museum's original dioramas portraying each bureau's history as well as artifacts, documents, photographs, and crafts. An Indian arts and crafts shop and many areas of the building containing artwork are open to the public. Other Interior Department offices in the Washington area are the Bureau of Mines and the U.S. Geological Survey.

Department of Justice

The Department of Justice had numerous homes before Congress appropriated $12 million for its permanent headquarters in downtown Washington. Under construction from 1931 to 1935, the Justice building fills the block of Federal Triangle between Ninth and Tenth streets, NW, and Constitution and Pennsylvania avenues.

The seven-story limestone structure comprises a gross floor area of 1.2 million square feet, including 1,712 rooms, 87 stairways, almost four miles of corridors, and underground parking for 150 cars. More than twenty-five hundred employees occupy the building.

Principal architects Clarence Zantzinger and Charles L. Borie, Jr., made wide use of aluminum, an uncommon construction material for that period. The exterior doors (each twenty feet tall), frames for the 1,908 windows, all door trim, stair railings, and much ornamentation are aluminum. One observer remarked that the designers used enough aluminum to make "not only forks and spoons but pots and pans for a whole city."

Although the exterior of the Justice headquarters, like many federal buildings, is classical revival in style, many of its decorative elements reflect the Art Deco influence of the 1920s and 1930s. Notable Art Deco features include the nine exterior doors and aluminum torchiers as well as John Joseph Earley's striking mosaic ceilings, the first made of American materials.

All sculptural work was designed by C. Paul Jennewein, who consulted philosophy professor Hartley B. Alexander in rendering a unified theme for the numerous exterior relief panels depicting the role of a justice department in a constitutional democracy. Still, his work aroused controversy. The president's Commission on Fine Arts objected to three nude male figures proposed for a six-by-fourteen-foot exterior relief panel and, in a letter to Jennewein, asked, "Do you think it would be possible to adopt the fig leaf for these figures?" Jennewein conceded and offered a second design. The commis-

Departmental Headquarters

sioners again objected: "The fig leaves are not quite large enough," they wrote. Today, the larger fig leaves may be seen in the pediment above the Constitution Avenue entrance.

Throughout the building, vast murals by noted New Deal artists Boardman Robinson, George Biddle, and John Steuart Curry depict themes of justice. The murals took six years to complete (1935-1941) and cost $68,000.

Other offices of the Justice Department include the Federal Bureau of Investigation and the Immigration and Naturalization Service in Washington and the U.S. Marshals Service in McLean, Virginia. The FBI building, across Pennsylvania Avenue from the department headquarters, offers tours that are a popular tourist attraction. The building is named for the bureau's first director, J. Edgar Hoover. *(FBI, p. 136)*

Department of Labor

The modern Department of Labor building, which occupies two city blocks at 200 Constitution Avenue, NW, was dedicated by President Gerald R. Ford upon its completion in 1974. Six years later President Jimmy Carter named the building for Franklin D. Roosevelt's labor secretary, Frances Perkins, on the centennial of her birth, April 10, 1980.

The six-story steel and limestone building, designed by two Texas architectural firms—Brooks, Barr, Graeber, and White of Austin, and Pitts, Mebane, Phelps, and White of Houston—comprises one million square feet of office space and two and one-half miles of corridors. It cost $95 million to build and houses forty-seven hundred employees. Like Health and Human Services, the Labor headquarters was built above a freeway tunnel, so the architects had to incorporate exhaust shafts into the building's design.

To commemorate the country's bicentennial in 1976, the General Services Administration commissioned New York artist Jack Beal to paint four murals for the building. Called "The History of Labor in America," the work continues the tradition of Social Realist art exemplified by the New Deal artists in other government buildings in Washington.

The Labor Department also occupies two other buildings in Washington and numerous regional and field offices, including eight regional offices of the Bureau of Labor Statistics and ten of the Occupational Safety and Health Administration.

Department of State

Until 1947 the State Department shared quarters with the War and Navy departments in the State, War, and Navy Building (now called the Old Executive Office Building) at Seventeenth Street and Pennsylvania Avenue, NW, next door

Executive Branch

to the White House. When the department needed more space, it moved to its current location at Twenty-first and D streets, NW. The eight-story, neoclassical limestone building was designed by Gilbert S. Underwood and William Dewey Foster; Louis A. Simon served as supervising architect.

The department continued to grow and by the mid-1950s—less than a decade after it moved—it occupied more than twenty-five annexes in addition to its main building. Congress approved funding for an extension, which was built from 1957 to 1961 under direction of the architectural firm of Graham, Anderson, Probst, and White.

The State Department building today covers 11.8 acres—the two blocks between Twenty-first and Twenty-third streets on the east and west and C and D streets on the south and north. The building contains approximately 2.5 million square feet of gross floor space and houses the Agency for International Development (AID) and the Arms Control and Disarmament Agency in addition to State Department staff, approximately seven thousand employees altogether. Other AID and State employees staff approximately two hundred fifty U.S. embassies, consulates, and missions in 155 countries around the world.

At the C Street entrance of the contemporary-styled addition is the three-story Diplomatic Lobby. Television reporters covering the State Department often broadcast from this room, where the national flags of countries that have diplomatic relations with the United States form a colorful backdrop. At each end of the lobby is a plaque commemorating more than one hundred fifty State Department employees who have died "under heroic or tragic circumstances in foreign service." More than seventy-five names have been added since 1965. The Exhibition Hall on the first floor displays the Great Seal of the United States, in use since 1782 to seal instruments of ratification of treaties and the commissions of cabinet officers, ambassadors, and Foreign Service officers.

In 1961 the State Department's Fine Arts Committee began the Americana Project to remodel and redecorate—entirely through private funds—the sixteen diplomatic reception rooms on the eighth floor and the office of the secretary. The refurnished rooms, a showcase of the country's cultural heritage, contain museum-quality furniture, rugs, paintings, and silver from the classical period of American design, 1740-1825. Senior government officials, including the president and secretary of state, use the rooms for official functions.

Department of Transportation

The Nassif Building, which contains the principal offices of the Transportation Department, is the only departmental headquarters not built and owned by the federal government. The General Services Administration, the federal government's property manager, leases 1.6 million square feet of the building, bounded by D, E, Sixth, and Seventh streets, SW, for $8.6 million a year.

Edward Durell Stone, architect of the Kennedy Center and the National Geographic Society building in Washington, designed the modern ten-story structure for Boston real estate developer David Nassif. When completed in 1969 it was the largest private office building in Washington. The one-inch white marble exterior veneer comes from quarries in Carrara, Italy, like the marble in the Kennedy Center.

The only major change or addition since Transportation first occupied the building in 1970 was the construction of a 22,873-square-foot computer room in 1983. Approximately fifty-five hundred of the department's more than eleven thousand employees work in the Nassif Building. Other Transportation offices in Washington include the headquarters of the Federal Aviation Administration and the Coast Guard.

Department of the Treasury

The Treasury building is the oldest federal government departmental headquarters. The five-story granite structure in the Greek Revival style set a precedent for the design of many other government buildings in Washington. Constructed in stages from 1836 through 1869, it is Treasury's third home on this site. The first Treasury building was burned by the British in 1814; the second, by arsonists in 1833.

Treasury's five wings fill two city blocks at Fifteenth Street and Pennsylvania Avenue, NW, just east of the White House. Legend has it that President Andrew Jackson, annoyed at the protracted controversy over the exact location of the building, one day walked over from the White House, planted his cane in the ground, and declared, "Right here is where I want the cornerstone." Unfortunately, the building spoiled the clear view along Pennsylvania Avenue between the White House and Capitol. Treasury served as a barracks for Union soldiers during the Civil War and provided a temporary office for President Andrew Johnson while he waited six weeks for Mary Todd Lincoln to leave the White House after her husband's assassination.

Robert Mills, architect of the Washington Monument, designed the east and center wings (1836-1842). The most impressive feature of Mills's design is the east front

Executive Branch

colonnade—thirty Ionic columns, each thirty-six feet (three stories) tall, carved from a single block of granite. Thomas Ustick Walter, architect of the Capitol dome, did the preliminary design of the west and south wings (1855-1864). Ammi B. Young and Isaiah Rogers completed the plans, incorporating ornate details of late nineteenth-century tastes in their interior designs.

The architect of the north wing (1867-1869) was Alfred Bult Mullett, designer of the State, War, and Navy Building, now known as the Old Executive Office Building. In the north wing is the Cash Room, a two-story hall finished in nine varieties of marble. The seventy-two by thirty-two foot room was opened in 1869, in time to serve as the site of President Ulysses S. Grant's inaugural ball March 4 of that year.

At 450,000 square feet (290,000 of which is office space), Treasury was one of the largest office buildings in the world when it was finished. Today the headquarters houses only 6 percent of the department's twenty thousand Washington-area employees. Others work in the Treasury Annex, connected to the main building by a tunnel under Pennsylvania Avenue, and in buildings housing the various bureaus of the department, including the Bureau of Printing and Engraving and the Internal Revenue Service. Treasury has field organizations in every state and offices in most major U.S. cities.

Department of Veterans Affairs

The goal of consolidating under one roof all Washington employees handling veterans affairs has eluded the federal government throughout most of the twentieth century. In the early 1900s the department's predecessor, the Bureau of War Risk Insurance, operated out of seventeen different buildings. In late 1988, when the Veterans Administration gained cabinet-level status, the new Department of Veterans Affairs (DVA) occupied eight buildings in the Washington metropolitan area. The main building, containing the office of the secretary, is at 810 Vermont Avenue, NW.

The eleven-story structure in the classical revival style was designed by the architectural firm of Wyatt and Nolting to be a hotel. In 1918, however, the government bought the site and foundation for $1 million, redesigned the exterior, and modified the interior to accommodate offices rather than hotel rooms. Construction of the War Risk Building, as it then was called, was completed in 1918 at a cost of $3.6 million. It comprises 442,000 square feet of office space. Today the building houses approximately twenty-nine hundred out of seven thousand DVA employees in the Washington area.

*Capital
Attractions*

Capital Attractions

Following are popular sightseeing attractions in Washington not described elsewhere in this volume.

Unless otherwise indicated, the museums of the Smithsonian Institution are open daily from 10:00 a.m. to 5:30 p.m. Extended spring and summer hours are determined annually. The Smithsonian is closed on Christmas.

Anacostia Museum

The Smithsonian's Anacostia Museum showcases the cultural contributions of Afro-Americans. It is located in the historic Anacostia section of Southeast Washington, at 1901 Fort Place, SE.

Subjects of exhibitions have included African-American inventors, black aviators, the Harlem Renaissance, and the development of African-American churches.

Reference materials are available for scholars in the Research Department.

For information about tours and programs, call (202) 287-3369 (voice) or (202) 357-1729 (TDD).

Arlington National Cemetery

The Arlington National Cemetery, across the Potomac River from Washington, D.C., in Virginia, is the final resting place for more than two hundred thousand veterans and their dependents. On the 612 acres of land are buried representatives from every war the United States has fought.

The mansion and estate that became the cemetery had been willed to Mary Custis, daughter of George Washington Parke Custis and wife of Robert E. Lee. When the Civil War became imminent, Lee resigned his commission in the U.S. Army and, with his family, left the estate. The federal government confiscated the property, using it as headquarters for the Army of the Potomac. By the end of the war, more than sixteen thousand soldiers were buried on the plantation.

Many prominent figures lie in Arlington Cemetery, including Pierre Charles L'Enfant, architect of Washington, D.C.; William Howard Taft, president and later chief justice of the United States; Robert E. Peary and Richard Byrd, arctic explorers; Joe Louis, world heavyweight boxing champion; and Dick Scobee and Michael Smith, astronauts on the space

Capital Attractions

shuttle *Challenger*. War heroes include Audie Murphy, John J. Pershing, George C. Marshall, Omar Bradley, and Daniel "Chappie" James.

Of particular interest are the Kennedy gravesites—those of President John F. Kennedy, with its eternal flame, and his brother Senator Robert F. Kennedy—and the Tomb of the Unknowns. Four unknown servicemen—from World War I, World War II, the Korean Conflict, and the Vietnam War—are interred at the tomb, which is guarded twenty-four hours a day by a soldier from the Army's U.S. 3d Infantry. The soldier takes twenty-one steps before turning and facing the tomb for twenty-one seconds. The changing of the guard ceremony takes place every hour on the hour from October 1 through March 31, and every half hour from April 1 through September 30.

Arlington is the largest of the more than one hundred national cemeteries in the United States. More than thirty-five hundred funerals are held in Arlington each year. The grounds are open daily from 8:00 a.m. to 5:00 p.m. October through March and from 8:00 a.m. to 7:00 p.m. April through September. The Lee-Custis mansion, or Arlington House, is open from 9:30 a.m. to 4:30 p.m. October through March and from 9:30 a.m. to 6:00 p.m. April through September.

Admission is free.

Arts and Industries Building

The largest installation of the National Museum of American History—"1876: A Centennial Exhibition"—is housed in the Arts and Industries building at 900 Jefferson Drive, SW, next door to the "Castle." Victorian America is evoked by this recreation of the exhibition held in Philadelphia.

The Arts and Industries building is the second oldest Smithsonian building on the Mall. President James A. Garfield's 1881 inaugural ball was held there.

Group tours are available by calling (202) 357-1481. The building is handicapped accessible.

The Discovery Theater, which presents performances for children, operates from October through June. Call (202) 357-1500 for information.

Bureau of Engraving and Printing

The Bureau of Engraving and Printing, at Fourteenth and C streets, SW, is the federal government's security printer. The bureau designs and manufactures U.S. currency, postage stamps, and Treasury obligations.

On the self-guided tour, which lasts about twenty minutes, visitors can watch high-speed presses print bills, at a rate of seven thousand sheets per hour. Tour guides are posted along

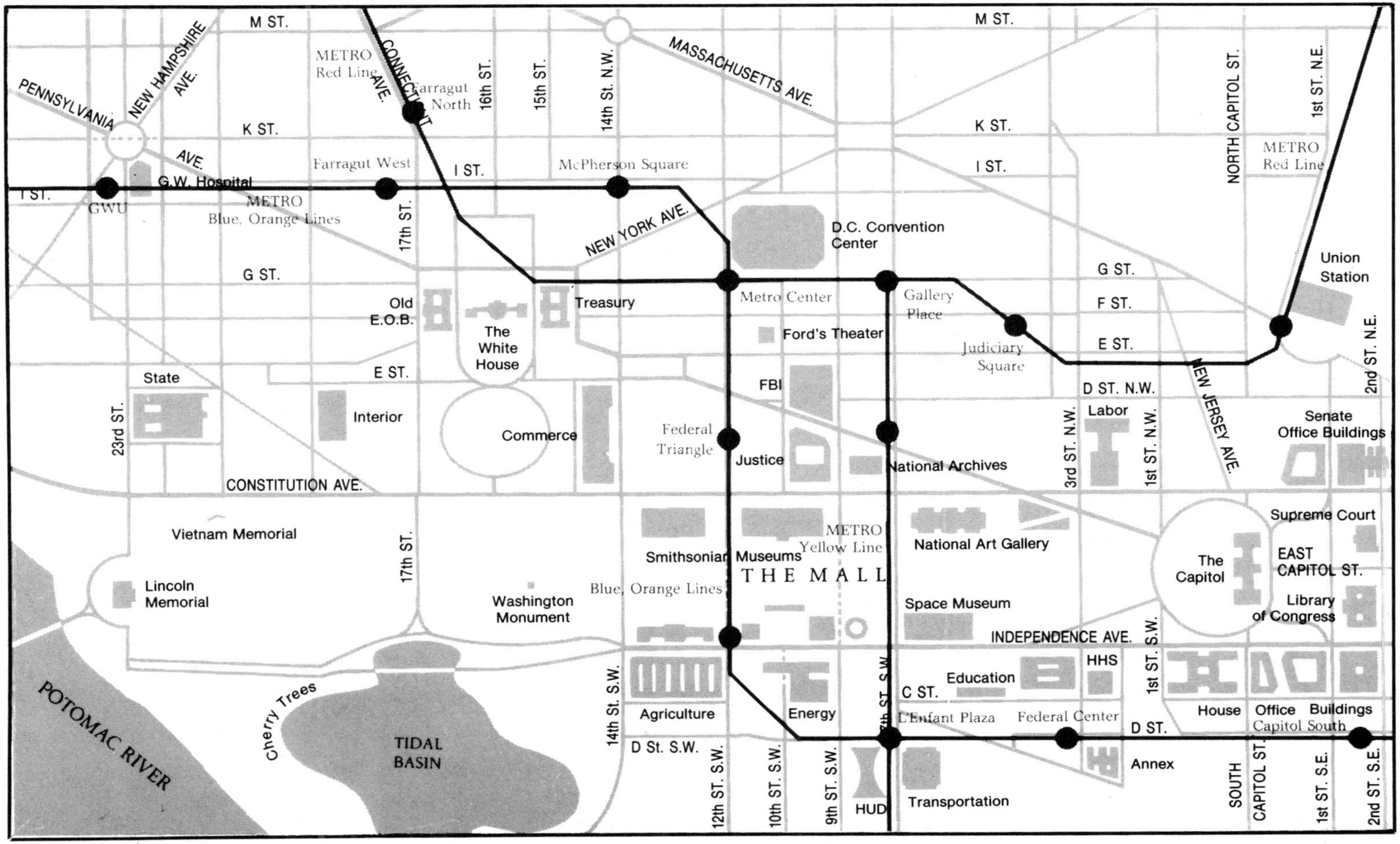
M ST.
NEW HAMPSHIRE AVE.
PENNSYLVANIA AVE.
K ST.
I ST.
GWU
G.W. Hospital
METRO
Blue, Orange Lines
METRO
Red Line
CONNECTICUT AVE.
Farragut North
Farragut West
16th ST.
15th ST.
14th St. N.W.
McPherson Square
17th ST.
MASSACHUSETTS AVE.
NEW YORK AVE.
D.C. Convention Center
G ST.
Old E.O.B.
The White House
Treasury
Metro Center
Gallery Place
Ford's Theater
Judiciary Square
F ST.
E ST.
State
23rd ST.
Interior
Commerce
FBI
Federal Triangle
Justice
National Archives
D ST. N.W.
Labor
3rd ST. N.W.
1st ST. N.W.
NEW JERSEY AVE.
NORTH CAPITOL ST.
1st ST. N.E.
Union Station
2nd ST. N.E.
Senate Office Buildings
CONSTITUTION AVE.
Vietnam Memorial
Lincoln Memorial
Washington Monument
Smithsonian Museums
METRO
Yellow Line
THE MALL
Blue, Orange Lines
National Art Gallery
Space Museum
The Capitol
Supreme Court
EAST CAPITOL ST.
Library of Congress
INDEPENDENCE AVE.
HHS
Education
C ST.
L'Enfant Plaza
Federal Center
D ST.
House
Office
Buildings
Capitol South
Annex
Agriculture
Energy
D St. S.W.
14th St. S.W.
12th ST. S.W.
10th ST. S.W.
9th ST. S.W.
7th ST. S.W.
HUD
Transportation
SOUTH CAPITOL ST.
1st ST. S.E.
2nd ST. S.E.
1st ST. S.W.
Cherry Trees
TIDAL BASIN
POTOMAC RIVER

Capital Attractions

the route to answer questions. Tours, available on a first-come, first-served basis, may be taken Monday through Friday from 9:00 a.m. to 2:00 p.m. The Visitors' Center, open from 8:30 a.m. to 2:30 p.m., has special exhibits. The bureau is closed for all federal holidays and during the week between Christmas and New Year's.

The bureau is a popular Washington attraction. Visitors are encouraged to arrive early during the peak tourist season, when the average wait is ninety minutes and the line has been known to be cut off as early as noon.

Photographs and smoking are prohibited inside the building. The bureau is wheelchair accessible.

Corcoran Gallery of Art

The Corcoran Gallery of Art is Washington's oldest and largest private gallery house. It has an extensive collection of American painting and sculpture and a more limited European collection.

The gallery, founded in 1869 by American financier, philanthropist, and art collector William Wilson Corcoran (1798-1888), first was located in what is today the Renwick Gallery. It moved to its present quarters, at Seventeenth Street and New York Avenue, NW, in 1897. The building was designed by Ernest Flagg.

The gallery is open from 10:00 a.m. to 4:30 p.m. on Tuesday, Wednesday, Friday, Saturday, and Sunday, and from 10:00 a.m. to 9:00 p.m. on Thursday. It is closed on Mondays, Christmas, and New Year's.

Admission is free. Group tours and handicapped facilities need to be arranged in advance; call (202) 638-1070.

An art school is affiliated with the gallery.

Federal Bureau of Investigation

The Federal Bureau of Investigation's J. Edgar Hoover building, on Pennsylvania Avenue between Ninth and Tenth streets, NW, is the third most popular tourist attraction in Washington.

The free one-hour tour shows visitors crime laboratories; displays of confiscated jewelry, furs, and guns; photos of fugitives who have been on the Ten Most Wanted list; and a live firearms demonstration.

The FBI headquarters is open for tours Monday through Friday, from 8:45 a.m. to 4:15 p.m., except on federal holidays. Visitors are encouraged to arrive early because the line forms quickly and the wait can be long. Passes for reserved times can be obtained through congressional offices or directly from the FBI. Reservations for group tours also can be made. Write

Capital Attractions

FBI Tour, Tenth Street and Pennsylvania Avenue, NW, Room M-596, Washington, D.C. 20535.

The building is wheelchair accessible.

Ford's Theatre

Abraham Lincoln, the sixteenth president of the United States, was shot by John Wilkes Booth April 14, 1865, during a production of *Our American Cousin* at Ford's Theatre. The mortally wounded president was taken across the street to the Petersen House—home of William Petersen, a tailor—where he died the next day at 7:22 a.m.

Today the theater, at 511 Tenth Street, NW, is both a memorial to Lincoln and a living theater. The Lincoln Museum is in the basement of the building, and the theater hosts a full schedule of plays during the year.

Ford's Theatre is open daily from 9:00 a.m. to 5:00 p.m., except on Christmas. The theater is closed to tours during rehearsals and matinees—usually on Thursday, Saturday, and Sunday—although the Lincoln Museum and Petersen House remain open.

A small fee is charged for the tour; admission is free for senior citizens, children under twelve, educational groups, and the handicapped. The theater is handicapped accessible.

Freer Gallery of Art

The Freer Gallery of Art, the Smithsonian's first art museum, closed for renovation in 1988 and is scheduled to reopen in 1992. The museum is located adjacent to the Arthur M. Sackler Gallery.

The Freer houses Asian and Near Eastern art from Neolithic times to the early twentieth century and American art from the late nineteenth and early twentieth centuries. It contains a significant collection of works by James McNeill Whistler, including his famous "Peacock Room."

Industrialist Charles Lang Freer (1854-1919) offered his private collection to the Smithsonian in 1905. The museum opened in 1923.

During the renovation, the gallery's staff will provide visiting scholars access to the gallery's collection. Make requests in advance by calling (202) 357-2104 or writing Freer Gallery of Art, Smithsonian Institution, Jefferson Drive at Twelfth Street, SW, Washington, D.C. 20560.

Enid A. Haupt Garden

The Enid A. Haupt Garden is situated on top of the Smithsonian's underground museum, education, and research complex—the S. Dillon Ripley Center, the Arthur M. Sackler Gallery, and the National Museum of African Art—at 1000

Capital Attractions

Independence Avenue, SW, behind the "Castle" and between the Freer Gallery of Art and the Arts and Industries building.

Named for its donor, Enid Annenberg Haupt, the garden features saucer magnolias, hybrid tea roses, Victorian embroidery parterre, and nineteenth-century garden furniture.

Hirshhorn Museum and Sculpture Garden

The Hirshhorn Museum and Sculpture Garden, designed by Gordon Bunshaft, is dedicated to contemporary art—nineteenth and twentieth century painting and sculpture. The heart of the permanent collection was a gift from philanthropist and financier Joseph H. Hirshhorn (1899-1981), a Latvian-born immigrant.

The museum, at Independence Avenue and Seventh Street, SW, is cylindrical in shape, 231 feet in diameter. It is built on four piers, fourteen feet above the ground. The garden, which is open daily from 7:30 a.m. to dusk, is adjacent to the museum.

Works of prominent artists on display include those by Henri Matisse, Auguste Rodin, Alexander Calder, Edgar Degas, Pablo Picasso, Edward Hopper, and Willem de Kooning.

Tours are given beginning at 10:30 a.m., noon, and 1:30 p.m. Monday through Saturday and at 12:30 p.m., 1:30 p.m., and 2:30 p.m. on Sunday. Group tours for students are available by appointment; call (202) 357-3235. Sculpture tours for the blind and visually impaired and sign-language tours also are available. Wheelchairs may be borrowed from the checkroom.

Strollers are not permitted in the galleries because they can damage low-hanging paintings. Visitors are allowed to use hand-held cameras inside the museum, but not flash or tripods.

Scholars may use the library, with its twelve thousand volumes, by appointment; call (202) 357-3222. For a schedule of events sponsored by the Hirshhorn, write Public Affairs, Hirshhorn Museum and Sculpture Garden, Washington, D.C. 20560.

Thomas Jefferson Memorial

The memorial to Thomas Jefferson—author of the Declaration of Independence, third president of the United States, and founder of the University of Virginia—is situated along the south bank of the Tidal Basin, directly across from the White House. The memorial is a pictorially familiar sight to most Americans because of the beautiful flowering cherry trees planted around the Tidal Basin that bloom in early spring. The trees were a gift from the city of Tokyo and were planted in 1912.

The memorial was designed by John Russell Pope, along

Capital Attractions

with Otto R. Eggers and Daniel P. Higgins. The cornerstone was officially laid November 15, 1938, and the building was dedicated April 12, 1943, the two-hundredth anniversary of Jefferson's birth.

Visitors enter the memorial from the Tidal Basin side. The sculpture group above the entranceway, created by Adolph A. Weinman, depicts the committee appointed by the Continental Congress to write the Declaration of Independence. Jefferson is standing with Benjamin Franklin and John Adams to the left and Roger Sherman and Robert R. Livingston seated to the right.

A nineteen-foot statue of Jefferson, sculpted by Rudulph Evans, stands at the center of the domed interior, on a pedestal of black Minnesota granite. On the interior walls, made of white Georgia marble, are four inscriptions from Jefferson's writings. The domed ceiling is made of Indiana limestone; the exterior walls and dome are made of Danby Imperial Vermont marble. A colonnade surrounds the building.

The memorial is open twenty-four hours a day. A National Park Service ranger is on duty from 8:00 a.m. to midnight, except on Christmas. No admission is charged. The building is wheelchair accessible.

John F. Kennedy Center for the Performing Arts

The Kennedy Center is both a memorial to John F. Kennedy, thirty-fifth president of the United States, and a performing arts center. The idea for a national cultural center to be located in Washington, D.C., was originated by George Washington.

The Kennedy Center, on New Hampshire Avenue at Rock Creek Parkway, NW, next door to the Watergate, was designed by Edward Durell Stone and cost approximately $78 million. The box-shaped structure is 630 feet long, 300 feet deep, and 100 feet high. Much of the building is constucted with Carrara marble, a gift from Italy.

The center features five theaters—the Eisenhower Theatre, the Opera House, the Concert Hall, the Terrace Theatre, and the American Film Insitute Theatre. In the Grand Foyer, one of the largest rooms in the world, is the Robert Berks bronze bust of President Kennedy. The Hall of States contains the flags of the fifty United States, and the Hall of Nations displays the flags of nations recognized diplomatically by the United States.

The Theatre Lab is used for experimental theater and children's theater. The Performing Arts Library, joint project of the Kennedy Center and the Library of Congress, keeps

Capital Attractions

scripts, recordings, and other performing arts-related information. The library is open from 11:00 a.m. to 8:30 p.m. Tuesday through Friday and from 10:00 a.m. to 6:00 p.m. on Saturday.

Guided tours, which last about forty-five minutes, are offered daily from 10:00 a.m to 1:00 p.m. and depart from Motor Lobby A. In the lobby, an introductory film is shown continuously. A brochure is available for visitors to conduct self-guided tours. The box offices are open from 10:00 a.m. to 9:00 p.m. Monday through Saturday and from noon to 9:00 p.m. on Sunday and holidays. To make arrangements for wheelchairs, call (202) 254-3774.

Lincoln Memorial

The Lincoln Memorial, a tribute to the sixteenth president of the United States, is situated at the west end of the Mall overlooking the Reflecting Pool.

Henry Bacon designed the Grecian temple-like structure. The exterior is made of white Colorado-Yule marble. The outer columns of the structure are Doric; the inner columns, Ionic. The columns total thirty-six, the number of states in the Union at the time of Lincoln's assassination. The names of these states are engraved in the frieze above the colonnade, and on the attic walls above the frieze are engraved the names of the forty-eight states that made up the United States in 1922, the year the memorial was dedicated. Ernest Bairstow carved the frieze and attic walls. An inscription on the terrace in front of the memorial notes the addition of Alaska and Hawaii in 1959.

Daniel Chester French designed the nineteen-foot statue of a seated Lincoln; the Piccirilli brothers carved it, with French's assistance. The statue is made of twenty-eight blocks of Georgia white marble and sits on a platform of Tennessee marble.

Two large insribed stone tablets hang in the memorial, each with a mural above it painted by Jules Guerin. On the north wall is Lincoln's Second Inaugural Address and a mural depicting the unity of the North and South. Figures symbolizing fraternity and charity are included on the left and right. On the south wall is Lincoln's Gettysburg Address and a mural depicting an angel freeing a slave. Figures symbolizing justice and immortality are included on the left and right.

The interior walls of the memorial are made of Indiana limestone. The floor and the wall base are made of pink Tennessee marble.

The memorial is open twenty-four hours a day. A National Park Service ranger is present from 8:00 a.m. to mid-

Capital Attractions

night, except on Christmas. No admission is charged, and the memorial is wheelchair accessible.

National Air and Space Museum

The National Air and Space Museum is one of the Smithsonian's most frequently visited museums—approximately nine million people annually. The twenty-three exhibit areas of the museum chronicle the evolution of air and space technology.

Displayed are airplanes, spacecraft, missiles, rockets, and other flight-related artifacts. Popular items include the Wright brothers' original 1903 flyer; Charles A. Lindbergh's "Spirit of St. Louis"; the Apollo 11 Command Module; and a Skylab Orbital Workshop, which visitors may enter. Unless otherwise noted, all aircraft and spacecraft displayed were actually flown or used as backups.

Featured in the museum, located on Independence Avenue between Fourth and Seventh streets, SW, are the Albert Einstein Planetarium and the Langley Theater. For a nominal fee, visitors to the planetarium can see *Calling All Stars*, which explores the possibility of extraterrestrial life. Various films are shown on the giant screen—five stories high and seven stories wide—of the Langley Theater: *To Fly!*, a bird's eye view of America; *The Dream Is Alive*, about the space shuttle program; *On the Wing*, a depiction of flight in all its forms; *Flyers*, a fictional account of the exploits of an American aviator; and *Living Planet*, an aerial travelog across five continents. A small admission is charged for each film.

Tours are given each day beginning at 10:15 a.m. and 1:00 p.m. Recorded tours, which may be rented, also are available in English and six foreign languages. For groups of twenty-five or more, theater, planetarium, and tour reservations may be made from three to eight weeks in advance. Write Tour Scheduler,

Capital Attractions

NASM, Washington, D.C. 20560. Tours for the handicapped also may be arranged; call (202) 357-1400. Wheelchairs are available, free of charge.

Visitors have access to the museum's research library, which contains twenty-four thousand books and journals, a rare book room, documents, and photographs. Check with the Information Desk on the first floor. The library is open Monday through Friday from 10:00 a.m. to 4:00 p.m.

National Aquarium

The National Aquarium is the oldest aquarium in the United States. It was founded in 1873 and was housed in a variety of locations until it found a permanent home in 1932 in the Department of Commerce building at Fourteenth Street and Constitution Avenue, NW.

Since 1980 the aquarium has been classified a nonprofit organization, and in 1982 the National Aquarium Society was founded to support and run the operation. In the aquarium's seventy-four tanks are more than twelve hundred specimens representing 250 species. The sharks are fed at 2:00 p.m. on Monday, Wednesday, and Saturday; the piranhas at 2:00 p.m. on Tuesday, Thursday, and Sunday.

As part of the exhibit are a Learning Center; a Touch Tank, which allows visitors to touch sea animals; and a Mini-Theatre, which continuously shows films on aquatic life. For a list of topics and speakers featured in the Lecture Series, write The National Aquarium, Department of Commerce Building, Room B-037, Washington, D.C. 20230 or call (202) 377-2826.

The aquarium is open every day, except Christmas, from 9:00 a.m. to 5:00 p.m. Admission is $2.00 for adults, 75¢ for children aged three to twelve and for senior citizens over sixty.

National Archives

The National Archives and Records Administration is home to the Charters of Freedom—the Declaration of Independence, the Constitution, and the Bill of Rights—which are on public display in the Exhibition Hall. What most visitors do not see, however, are the 3.2 billion textual documents, 1.6 million cartographic items, 5.2 million still photographs, 9.7 million aerial photographs, 110,000 reels of film, and 173,000 video and sound recordings that make up the permanent valuable records of the U.S. government that the archives is instructed to preserve and make available for reference and research.

The stately National Archives, at Seventh Street and Constitution Avenue, NW, was designed by John Russell Pope, who also designed the Jefferson Memorial and the National

Capital Attractions

Gallery of Art West Building. Construction began in 1932 and was finished in 1937, at cost of more than $12 million. The bronze doors at the Constitution Avenue entrance each weigh 6.5 tons and are 38 feet 7 inches high, about 10 feet wide, and 11 inches thick.

The Charters of Freedom are exhibited in a protective glass encasement in the Circular Gallery that runs along the back of the Exhibition Hall, or Rotunda. On either side of the case are displayed the two sides of the Great Seal of the United States; on the left the obverse, on the right the reverse. At night and during emergencies, the case is lowered into a fifty-five-ton vault made of reinforced steel and concrete.

Two murals by Barry Faulkner (1881-1966) hang in the hall. On the left is "The Declaration of Independence," depicting Thomas Jefferson presenting a draft to the Continental Congress; on the right is "The Constitution," depicting James Madison submitting the Constitution to the Constitutional Convention. Four winged, bronze figures—representing legislation, justice, history, and war and defense—help make up the floor design in the hall.

The National Archives also has on indefinite display a copy of the Magna Carta, which is on loan from its owner, Dallas businessman H. Ross Perot.

The Exhibition Hall, entered from the Constitution Avenue side of the building, is open daily from 10:00 a.m. to 9:00 p.m., April 1 through Labor Day, and from 10:00 a.m. to 5:30 p.m., the day after Labor Day to March 31. It is closed on Christmas. Guided tours may be arranged in advance through the Office of Public Programs; call (202) 523-3183.

The Central Research and Microfilm Research Rooms, which are reached through the Pennsylvania Avenue entrance, are open from 8:45 a.m. to 10:00 p.m., Monday through Friday, and from 9:00 a.m. to 5:00 p.m. on Saturday. They are closed on federal holidays.

The building is handicapped accessible, and admission is free.

National Building Museum

The National Building Museum is devoted to recognizing American achievements in architecture and encouraging excellence in the building arts.

The building was designed by Montgomery C. Meigs, and its first tenant was the Pension Bureau (1885-1926). The stately and striking Great Hall, measuring 316 feet by 116 feet, has been the site of inaugural balls since 1885. The terra cotta frieze, depicting six Civil War military units repeated around

Capital Attractions

the exterior of the building, is 1,200 feet long and 3 feet high and was designed by Caspar Buberl.

The privately funded museum opened in 1985. It offers a variety of educational programs and exhibitions on architecture and engineering, urban planning, historic preservation, construction techniques, and building trades. Each May the museum hosts the Festival of the Building Arts during which artisans demonstrate their crafts. Monthly from September through June, noontime concerts are held free of charge.

Tours of the museum, located on F Street between Fourth and Fifth streets, NW, are given Tuesday through Friday at 12:30 p.m., on Saturday at 12:30 p.m. and 1:30 p.m., and on Sunday and holidays at 12:30 p.m. Group tours are available by reservation and handicapped facilities must be arranged in advance; call (202) 272-2448. Exhibition hours are 10:00 a.m. to 4:00 p.m., Monday through Saturday, and noon to 4:00 p.m., Sunday and holidays. The museum is closed Thanksgiving, Christmas, and New Year's.

National Gallery of Art

The National Gallery of Art West Building houses European paintings and sculpture from the thirteenth through nineteenth centuries and American art. The East Building has twentieth-century art and special exhibitions.

The nucleus of the permanent collection on display in the West Building was a gift from Andrew W. Mellon (1855-1937), financier and secretary of state (1921-1932). Funds from the A. W. Mellon Educational and Charitable Trust paid for construction of the building. The collection and the building were accepted by President Franklin D. Roosevelt on behalf of the United States in 1941.

John Russell Pope, architect of the Jefferson Memorial and the National Archives, designed the West Building. It is 785 feet long and has more than one hundred thousand square feet of exhibit area. It is one of the largest marble structures in the world. The exterior is rose-white Tennessee marble; the columns in the Rotunda were quarried in Tuscany, Italy; and the floor of the Rotunda is green marble from Vermont and gray marble from Tennessee.

The museum depends upon private donations for its collections. Of particular note in the West Building are Rembrandt's "Self-Portrait" and Leonardo da Vinci's "Ginevra de' Benci."

The East Building was designed by I. M. Pei and Architects as two connected triangular sections to fit the trapezoid-shaped piece of land on which it sits. Construction costs were paid by the son and daughter of Andrew Mellon—Paul Mellon

Capital Attractions

East Building

and the late Alisa Mellon Bruce—and by the Andrew W. Mellon Foundation. The same rose-white marble from Tennessee used for the West Building was used to contruct the East Building. A plaza is situated between the two buildings, and an underground walkway links them.

The East Building, which opened in 1978, contains works by Henri Matisse and Jackson Pollock, as well as a giant mobile by Alexander Calder.

The National Gallery of Art is on Constitution Avenue between Third and Seventh streets, NW. It is open every day except Christmas and New Year's. Operating hours are 10:00 a.m. to 5:00 p.m. Monday through Saturday and noon to 9:00 p.m. on Sunday. Extended summer hours are determined annually. Admission is free.

Visitors are allowed to take personal photographs using hand-held cameras, with flash, in the galleries, unless specifically prohibited. Parcels, briefcases, knapsacks, and umbrellas are not allowed in the exhibition areas; checkrooms are available. Pens with fluid ink are not allowed to be used in the galleries.

The museums are handicapped accessible. Wheelchairs and strollers can be obtained at the entrances.

National Geographic Society, Explorers Hall

The Explorers Hall, in the National Geographic Society's headquarters at Seventeenth and M streets, NW, displays exhibits of expeditions in anthropology and oceanography and explorations of outer space.

Capital Attractions

A number of interactive exhibits keep visitors entertained. A new globe, eleven feet in diameter, was installed in acknowledgment of the society's one-hundredth year, celebrated in 1988.

The hall is open Monday through Saturday, and on holidays, from 9:00 a.m. to 5:00 p.m. and on Sunday from 10:00 a.m. to 5:00 p.m. It is closed on Christmas.

The building is wheelchair accessible, and admission is free.

National Museum of African Art

The National Museum of African Art, at 950 Independence Avenue, SW, is the only museum in the United States exclusively devoted to the traditional arts of sub-Saharan Africa.

The museum was founded in 1964 by Warren M. Robbins as a private educational institution. It became a part of the Smithsonian in 1979 and was renamed the National Museum of African Art in 1981. Today it is housed in the underground complex of museums near the "Castle." The ground-level entrance pavilion is in the Enid A. Haupt Garden, directly across from the entrance to the Arthur M. Sackler Gallery.

The museum's calendar contains information about tours, lectures, and special events. A copy can be obtained from the Information Desk or by writing Public Affairs Office, National Museum of African Art, Smithsonian Institution, Washington, D.C. 20560. For reserved tours, call (202) 357-2700 (voice) or (202) 357-1729 (TDD).

Visitors are permitted to take pictures in the galleries, unless specifically prohibited. Flash is not allowed. Permission to use a tripod must be obtained from the Public Affairs Office.

The Eliot Elisonfon Photographic Archives has an extensive collection of color slides, black-and-white photographs, feature films, and unedited footage on African art and culture. The archives is open Monday through Friday, from 10:00 a.m. to 4:00 p.m., by appointment only; call (202) 357-4654.

The Warren M. Robbins Library, with more than fifteen thousand volumes, is open Monday through Friday, from 10:00 a.m. to 5:00 p.m., also by appointment; call (202) 357-4875.

Elevators are handicapped accessible, wheelchairs are available.

National Museum of American Art

The National Museum of American Art, part of the Smithsonian Institution, attempts to represent through its collection the entire range of America's artistic heritage—from colonial to contemporary times, from masters to lesser known artists, from those working at home to those working abroad.

Of special interest at the museum are the Lincoln Gallery, site of Abraham Lincoln's second inaugural reception; an extensive study of Native Americans and their culture by artist-anthropologist George Catlin; and works by such notables as Charles Willson Peale, Gilbert Stuart, Thomas Cole, Winslow Homer, Mary Cassatt, Albert Pinkham Ryder, James McNeill Whistler, Edward Hopper, Franz Kline, and Robert Rauschenberg.

Guided tours are given at noon Monday through Friday and at 2:00 p.m. on Saturday and Sunday. Reservations are required for group tours; call (202) 357-3111. For sign language or oral interpreters, call (202) 357-3111 (voice) or (202) 357-1696 (TDD) at least three days in advance of visit. A monthly calendar of events is available from the Office of Public Affairs, Room 182, National Museum of American Art, Smithsonian Institution, Washington, D.C. 20560. The museum and its restroom facilities are handicapped accessible.

The museum is located at Eighth and G streets, NW, in the same building as the National Portrait Gallery and the Archives of American Art. The Renwick Gallery (see below) and the Barney Studio House operate under the auspices of the National Museum of American Art. The Barney Studio House, at 2306 Massachusetts Avenue, NW, was built in 1902 and was home, studio, and salon to Alice Pike Barney. It is open by appointment only; call (202) 357-3111.

National Museum of American History

The Smithsonian's National Museum of American History collects, exhibits, and studies artifacts of American science, technology, and culture.

The museum features objects from a variety of subject areas, including medicine, transportation, agriculture, music, photography, stamps, coins, graphic arts, ceramics, glass, national pastimes, armed forces history, and political history. Of particular interest to visitors are the original Star-Spangled Banner, the Foucault pendulum, the chairs used by television's Edith and Archie Bunker of "All in the Family," a pair of ruby slippers worn by Judy Garland in the *Wizard of Oz*, and the gowns of the nation's first ladies. Other items of note in the permanent collection are the patent model of Eli Whitney's cotton gin, the original Ford Model T, a John Bull locomotive, and Alexander Graham Bell's original experimental telephones.

The museum is located at Fourteenth Street and Constitu-

Capital Attractions

Dining at Mall-Area Museums ...

The **Hirshhorn Museum and Sculpture Garden** runs an outdoor cafe, the Plaza Cafe, during summer only. It serves moderately priced sandwiches and salads.

Three restaurants and one cafeteria can be found on the upper level of the **John F. Kennedy Center for the Performing Arts**. The Roof Terrace Restaurant is open from 11:30 a.m. to 3:00 p.m. for lunch Monday through Friday and on weekend matinee days, from 5:30 to 9:30 p.m. for dinner daily, and from 9:30 p.m. to midnight for supper Tuesday through Saturday. The Hors d'Oeuvrerie offers cocktails and light fare from 5:00 p.m. to one or two hours after the last performance curtain. The Curtain Call Cafe is open daily from 5:00 to 9:00 p.m. The Encore Cafeteria is open daily from 11:00 a.m. to 8:00 p.m. The Roof Terrace Restaurant accepts reservations; call (202) 416-8555.

The popular **National Air and Space Museum** hosts two eateries—the Flight Line Cafeteria and the Wright Place Restaurant—located in a futuristic crystal palace at the east end of the building. The cafeteria, open daily from 10:00 a.m. to 5:00 p.m., is casual; the restaurant, situated above the cafeteria, is the most formal of the Smithsonian's restaurants. It is open daily from 11:30 a.m. to 3:00 p.m. and accepts credit cards. For reservations call (202) 371-8777.

The **National Aquarium**, in the Department of Commerce building, runs a cafeteria that serves lunch Monday through Friday from 9:00 a.m. to 2:00 p.m.

The **National Gallery of Art** offers visitors a choice of four places to dine. The **West Building**'s Garden Cafe, on the ground floor, has a sidewalk cafe-like atmosphere. The limited menu includes pasta dishes, entrees of fish and chicken, and simple desserts. The cafe is open from 11:00 a.m. to 4:00 p.m. Monday through Saturday—beverage and dessert service only from 4:00 to 4:30 p.m.—and from 11:00 a.m. to 7:00 p.m. on Sunday. Enter from Seventh Street after the gallery has closed. Large groups will be seated at 11:30 a.m. only. For reservations call (202) 347-9401. Charge cards are accepted.

The Terrace Cafe is on the upper level of the **East Building**. The menu, similar to the Garden Cafe's, includes an interesting Philadelphia salad and a fruit, cheese, and bread plate. The cafe is open from 11:00 a.m. to 4:00 p.m.

... From Fast Foods to Formal

Monday through Saturday and from noon to 4:00 p.m. on Sunday. Large groups can be accommodated at 11:30 a.m. only. For reservations call (202) 347-9401. Charge cards are accepted.

In the underground plaza between the two buildings are the Concourse Buffet and Cascade Cafe. The buffet is more casual and less expensive than the National Gallery's cafes. The Cascade Cafe's fare is like the Garden Cafe's. The buffet is open from 10:00 to 11:00 a.m. for coffee and pastries and from 11:00 a.m. to 4:00 p.m. for lunch on Monday through Saturday. It is open from 11:00 a.m. to 5:15 p.m. for lunch and from 5:15 to 5:50 p.m. for dessert and beverages on Sunday. The cafe is open from 11:00 a.m. to 3:30 p.m. on Saturday and Sunday in winter. Credit cards are accepted.

The Patent Pending Cafe at the **National Museum of American Art** serves breakfast from 10:00 to 10:30 a.m. and lunch from 11:00 a.m. to 3:30 p.m. Monday through Friday. It is open from 11:00 a.m. to 3:30 p.m. on Saturday and Sunday.

Visitors select what they would like to eat from a rotating carousel at the Cafeteria Carousel in the **National Museum of American History**. The cafeteria, on the lower level, is open daily from 10:00 to 11:00 a.m. for breakfast and from 11:00 a.m. to 5:00 p.m. for lunch and snacks. Also located in the museum, on the first floor, is the Victorian Ice Cream Parlour, which serves light lunches and dessert. It is open from 11:00 a.m. to 4:00 p.m. daily. Reservations may be made for large groups; call (202) 357-1832. Credit cards are accepted.

The **National Museum of Natural History**'s cafeteria has basic fast-food offerings. Located on the first floor of the museum, it is open daily from 10:00 to 11:00 a.m. for breakfast and from 11:00 a.m. to 5:00 p.m. for lunch and snacks.

The Pavilion at the **Old Post Office**, open 10:00 a.m. to 9:30 p.m. daily, has shopping-mall-like booths selling a wide variety of food as well as several sit-down restaurants.

Off the Mall, at the **National Zoological Park**, concession stands, with names such as Panda Cafe, provide visitors with a quick bite.

Capital Attractions

tion Avenue, NW. Times and topics of regular tours, lectures, demonstrations, and other activities are posted at the Information Desks. For special school and adult tours, for October through May only, call (202) 357-1481. TDD for the hearing impaired, call (202) 357-1563. Wheelchairs are available from the checkrooms; most restrooms are handicapped accessible. Visitors are allowed to use hand-held cameras, with flash, unless specifically prohibited.

National Museum of Health and Medicine

The National Museum of Health and Medicine of the Armed Forces Institute of Pathology was born out of the Civil War as doctors tried to find the sources of various diseases that were killing more soldiers than enemy fire.

The museum—with its extensive archive of documents, photographs, specimens, and artifacts—chronicles the nation's medical heritage. Researchers found the cause of yellow fever, developed the first successful vaccine against typhoid, and performed the autopsies on assassinated presidents Abraham Lincoln and James A. Garfield.

Located on the Walter Reed Army Medical Center campus at 6825 Sixteenth Street, NW, the museum is open from 9:30 a.m. to 4:30 p.m. Monday through Friday and from 11:30 a.m. to 4:30 p.m. Saturday, Sunday, and holidays. It is closed Thanksgiving, Christmas Eve, Christmas Day, New Year's Eve, and New Year's Day. Group tours are available by appointment; call (202) 576-2348 or write National Museum of Health and Medicine, Armed Forces Institute of Pathology, Washington, D.C. 20306. Access to the historical and anatomical study collections and to the Otis Historical Archives also is by appointment only. Telephone and mail inquires to the archives are accepted.

Photography, without flash, is permitted. The museum is handicapped accessible.

National Museum of Natural History

The National Museum of Natural History, at Tenth Street and Constitution Avenue, NW, displays specimens from the natural world—plants, animals, fossils, gems, minerals, rocks, and meteorites—and objects made by its inhabitants.

Exhibits explain the dynamics of evolution, the early history of mankind, and the development of world cultures. Highlights include the skeletons of dinosaurs, the moon rocks, and the 45.5-carat Hope Diamond.

Housed in the museum, which is part of the Smithsonian Institution, are a living coral reef and the Insect Zoo. In the Discovery Room, visitors of all ages may examine and handle objects from the collections. The Naturalist Center, for those over age twelve, provides guidance, reference, and study collections.

Posted in the Rotunda, on the first floor on the Mall side of the building, is information about exhibitions, lectures, demonstrations, and so on. A quarterly calendar of events can be obtained by writing the Office of Education, National Museum of Natural History, #158, Washington, D.C. 20560. Tours are available, September through June, at 10:30 a.m. and 1:30 p.m. Recorded tours for some exhibits are available for a nominal fee from the Audio Tour Desk in the Rotunda.

The Discovery Room is open Monday through Thursday from noon to 2:30 p.m. and Friday through Sunday from 10:30 a.m. to 3:30 p.m. On weekends and holidays, tickets, available at no charge, are required for admission to the Discovery Room.

The Naturalist Center is open Monday through Saturday from 10:30 a.m. to 4:00 p.m. and Sunday from noon to 5:00 p.m.

The Constitution Avenue entrance is wheelchair accessible.

National Portrait Gallery

The Smithsonian's National Portrait Gallery, at Eighth and F streets, NW, is found within the restored landmark Old Patent Office Building, along with the National Museum of American Art and the Archives of American Art.

The gallery contains portraits of more than seven hundred Americans who have made significant political, military, scientific, and cultural contributions. Of particular interest are the Hall of Presidents, the *Time* magazine cover collection, a series of Mathew Brady photographs, and a portrait of Mary Cassatt by Edgar Degas.

Tours are given Monday through Friday from 10:00 a.m. to 3:00 p.m. and on Saturday, Sunday, and holidays from 11:00 a.m. to 2:00 p.m. Reservations for group tours or tours on a special subject can be made by calling (202) 357-2920. Arrangements for sign language and oral interpreters should be made at least three days in advance. Call (202) 357-1697 (voice) or (202) 357-1696 (TDD).

Visitors may photograph objects owned by the National Portrait Gallery if the photos are for personal use only and are made with cameras using guarded flash or high-speed film, at a distance of six feet or more. Visitors may not photograph objects in special exhibits or objects on loan to the gallery.

Capital Attractions

National Zoological Park

The National Zoological Park was created by an act of Congress in 1889 and became a part of the Smithsonian in 1890. Plans for the zoo were draw up by Samuel Langley, third secretary of the Smithsonian; William Temple Hornaday, conservationist and head of the Smithsonian's vertebrate division; and Frederick Law Olmsted, noted landscape architect.

The zoo has moved over the years from exhibiting animals as individuals to having them live in natural groupings. The present goal is to make the zoo a biological park—combining in displays plants, animals, museum specimens, and art—to show the interdependence of life.

In addition to the more than four thousand animals it showcases—including Ling-Ling and Hsing-Hsing, the two giant pandas from China—the zoo runs research, education, and conservation programs. The ZOOlab (in the Education Building), the BIRDlab (in the Bird House), and the HERPlab (in the Reptile House) offer free activities for families to learn about the zoo and its animals. The Invertebrate Exhibit is dedicated to the study of the earth's earliest forms of life. It is open Thursday through Sunday. During peak visiting times, reservations may be made at the front desk of the Invertebrate Exhibit. For information about the free films that are regularly shown in the Education Building Auditorium or lectures, concerts, and other special events held at the zoo, call (202) 673-4717.

Strollers may be rented, for a small fee and deposit, daily from May 1 through August 31 and on weekends during the remaining months. Pets are not allowed in the zoo, but animals assisting the handicapped are permitted. Rules prohibit bike riding in the zoo, but bike racks are provided.

The main pedestrian and vehicular entrances to the zoo are located on the 3000 block of Connecticut Avenue, NW. The zoo also can be entered from Beach Drive and at the junction of Harvard Street and Adams Mill Road.

From May 1 to September 15, the grounds are open from 8:00 a.m. to 8:00 p.m., and the buildings are open from 9:00 a.m. to 6:00 p.m. From September 16 to April 30, the grounds are open from 8:00 a.m. to 6:00 p.m., and the buildings from 9:00 a.m. to 4:30 p.m.

Old Post Office

The Old Post Office building, completed in 1899, survived a number of serious threats of demolition only to be restored, revived, and, eventually, rededicated in 1983. The Old Post Office and its adjacent plazas, at Pennsylvania Avenue and Twelfth Street, NW, have been named the Nancy Hanks

Capital Attractions

Center in honor of the chairperson of the National Endowment of the Arts from 1969 to 1977.

The Old Post Office, done in Richardson Romanesque style, was home to the U.S. Postal Service until 1934. It was Washington's first steel frame structure, and it was the first building to have installed an electric power plant. The interior courtyard is one of the largest uninterrupted interior spaces in the city, measuring 184 feet long, 99 feet wide, and 160 feet high.

The 315-foot clock tower provides a breathtaking view of the city. Visitors also may inspect the ten Congress Bells given to the United States in 1976 by the Ditchley Foundation of Great Britain. The bells range in weight from 581 to 2,953 pounds and are replicas of the bells at Westminster Abbey in London. The tower is open from 8:00 a.m. to 11:00 p.m. from April through September and from 10:00 a.m. to 6:00 p.m. from October through March.

In addition to the federal offices housed in the building today, the Pavilion provides a variety of eateries and shops, as well as live entertainment. It is open from 10:00 a.m. to 9:30 p.m. daily.

Admission is free, and the building is handicapped accessible.

Renwick Gallery

The Renwick Gallery of the National Museum of American Art promotes the creative achievements of American designers and craftspeople.

The gallery showcases two rooms—the Octagon Room and the Grand Salon—that are furnished in the styles of the 1860s and 1870s. Crafts on exhibit and on sale in the Museum Shop include works made of glass, ceramic, wood, fiber, and metal.

The gallery, at Seventeeth Street and Pennsylvania Avenue, NW, was designed in 1859 in the French Second Empire style as the Corcoran Gallery of Art. It was renamed after its architect, James Renwick, Jr., in 1965 when it was transferred to the Smithsonian for restoration.

Tours are available, by appointment, at 10:00 a.m., 11:00 a.m., and 1:00 p.m.; call (202) 357-2531. Special programs also can be arranged for school or adult groups. A monthly calendar of events is available from the Office of Public Affairs, Room 182, National Museum of American Art, Smithsonian Institution, Washington, D.C. 20560. Permission is required to take photographs inside the building; call (202) 357-2531.

A handicapped entrance is located on Pennsylvania Ave-

Capital Attractions

nue at the Seventeenth Street corner. Wheelchairs are available.

S. Dillon Ripley Center

The S. Dillon Ripley Center is part of the three-level underground museum, education, and research complex situated near the "Castle." The center, at 1100 Jefferson Drive, SW, houses administrative offices of Smithsonian programs as well as the International Center, which features exhibits on world cultures.

S. Dillon Ripley served as the eighth secretary of the Smithsonian Institution.

Arthur M. Sackler Gallery

The Arthur M. Sackler Gallery displays Asian and Near Eastern art. The core of the gallery's collection was a gift from Arthur M. Sackler (1913-1987), a medical researcher, publisher, and art collector.

Visitors enter the museum, at 1050 Independence Avenue, SW, through a ground-level pavilion in the Enid A. Haupt Garden, directly across from the entrance to the National Museum of African Art. The exhibition areas are located on three underground levels.

Tours are offered daily at 11:30 a.m. Reservations for group tours must be made in writing at least three weeks in advance: Tours, Arthur M. Sackler Gallery, Smithsonian Institution, Washington, D.C. 20560. Sign language and oral interpreters are available with at least three days' notice. Call (202) 357-1697 (voice) or (202) 357-1696 (TDD).

Hand-held cameras with flash are permitted except in designated areas. Strollers are allowed in all galleries except crowded special exhibits. The building is wheelchair accessible, and wheelchairs are available at the entrance pavilion.

A library with approximately forty-five thousand volumes, more than two hundred periodicals, eight thousand photographs, and fifty thousand slides is open to the public Monday through Friday from 10:00 a.m. to 5:00 p.m. Call (202) 357-2091 for information.

To obtain a bimonthly calendar of events, write: Calendar, Arthur M. Sackler Gallery, Smithsonian Institution, Washington, D.C. 20560.

Smithsonian Institution Building

The "Castle," at 1000 Jefferson Drive, SW, was the Smithsonian Institution's first building. It was designed by James Renwick, Jr., and completed in 1855.

The Castle today is home to the Smithsonian Information Center, where visitors may obtain information about the

Capital Attractions

Smithsonian Institution "Castle"

Smithsonian's fourteen museums and zoo; administrative offices; and the Woodrow Wilson International Center for Scholars.

Union Station

The beautifully restored Union Station, at 40 Massachusetts Avenue, NE, is more than a stop for Amtrak or Metro. It is home to a variety of stores, restaurants, and movie theaters. The historic landmark first was completed in 1908.

The station is open from 10:00 a.m. to 9:00 p.m. Monday through Saturday and from noon to 6:00 p.m. on Sunday. It is closed Christmas, Thanksgiving, Easter, and New Year's.

U.S. National Arboretum

The purpose of the National Arboretum, established by an act of Congress in 1927, is to educate the public and conduct research on trees and shrubs.

Nine miles of paved roads provide access to the plantings

Capital Attractions

in the 444-acre arboretum. Of special interest are the azalea plantings, among the most extensive in the country; the National Bonsai Collection; the Gotelli Dwarf Conifer Collection; and the National Herb Garden.

Guided tours are available. Groups should make arrangements in advance by calling (202) 475-4815 or writing United States National Arboretum, 3501 New York Avenue, NE, Washington, D.C. 20002.

The arboretum is located in the Northeast section of Washington, bounded by Bladensburg Road, New York Avenue, M Street, and the Anacostia River. The visitors' entrance is on New York Avenue. The arboretum is open from 8:00 a.m. to 5:00 p.m. Monday through Friday and from 10:00 a.m. to 5:00 p.m. Saturday and Sunday. The Administration Building is open from 8:00 a.m. to 4:30 p.m. Monday through Friday and for scheduled events on Saturday and Sunday. The National Bonsai Collection is open daily from 10:00 a.m. to 2:30 p.m.

Visitors may bring pets on leashes and are allowed to picnic in designated areas. Bike riding and other recreational activities are prohibited. The greenhouses are not open to the public.

U.S. Naval Observatory

When the Naval Observatory was created in 1830, it was called the Depot of Charts and Instruments and situated in Foggy Bottom. Its mission then was to care for the navy's chronometers, charts, and other navigational equipment. In 1844 its role was expanded, it was reestablished as the U.S. Naval Observatory, and it was relocated to where the Lincoln Memorial now stands. In 1893 the observatory moved again to its present site at Thirty-fourth Street and Massachusetts Avenue, NW. The new buildings were designed by Richard Morris Hunt.

Today the observatory's mission includes determining the positions and motions of the Earth, sun, moon, planets, and stars; measuring the Earth's rotation; and maintaining the Master Clock for the United States. The largest telescope on the grounds is a twenty-six-inch refractor acquired in 1873. It was with this telescope, the largest of its kind in the world when installed, that the two satellites of Mars were discovered in 1877 by Asaph Hall. Additional observatory telescopes are maintained in Flagstaff, Arizona, and Black Birch, New Zealand.

Free nighttime tours, which include viewing through telescopes and discussions with staff astronomers, are offered at

Capital Attractions

various times. Telescopes are not available during the day, when overcast, or on federal holidays. Groups should make reservations. Call (202) 653-1543 or write U.S. Naval Observatory, Thirty-fourth Street and Massachusetts Avenue, NW, Washington, D.C. 20392.

For the precise time, call (202) 653-1800. The time also is available commercially by dialing (900) 410-TIME.

Vietnam Veterans Memorial

The Vietnam Veterans Memorial, located between the Lincoln Memorial and Constitution Garden, honors the men and women of the armed forces who served in the Vietnam War.

The entrance plaza showcases a life-size sculpture of three soldiers, designed by Frederick Hart, and an American flag flying from a sixty-foot staff, the base of which has the emblems of the five services.

The V-shaped wall, designed by Maya Ying Lin, is made of highly reflective black granite and is inscribed with a chronological listing of the 58,132 casualties, missing in action (MIA), and prisoners of war (POW). Preceding (on the west wall) or following (on the east wall) each individual's name is a diamond or a cross. The diamond means the person's death was confirmed; the cross means the person was either missing or a prisoner at the end of the war. Approximately thirteen hundred names on the wall are accompanied with a cross. If a person returns alive, a circle is inscribed around the cross. If an MIA or POW is confirmed dead, a diamond is superimposed over the cross.

The personal nature of the design of the memorial and its quiet setting promote contemplation and reflection. Visitors commonly are seen making rubbings of names on the wall. Mementos and tokens of remembrance often are left. Books are available to aid in locating names on the wall.

The memorial's walls, which point to the Washington Monument and the Lincoln Memorial, are 246.75 feet long, and the angle at the vortex is 125° 12'. The highest point on the wall is 10.1 feet. The granite comes from Bangalore, India, and was cut and fabricated at Barre, Vermont. The names were grit-blasted in Memphis, Tennessee.

Establishing the memorial was the idea of Vietnam veteran Jan Scruggs. The walls were completed in October 1982, and the memorial was dedicated November 13, 1982. The sculpture was installed in late 1984. The memorial cost approximately $7 million, which was raised through private contributions.

Capital Attractions

Washington Monument

The Washington Monument stands at the center of the Mall as a tribute to George Washington, commander in chief of the Continental Army, president of the Constitutional Convention, and first president of the United States.

Construction of the monument began in 1848, based on an elaborate design by Robert Mills that featured a decorated obelisk. Over the next thirty-seven years, until the structure was completed in 1885, the design underwent radical transformations to conform to the traditional concept of obelisks.

For a period of twenty-five years construction stood at a standstill. When it resumed, new Maryland marble was obtained from the same vein as the marble used for the lower part of the structure. However, it came from a different stratum, and, as a result, the shaft has a noticeable ring.

The monument opened to the public in 1888. Visitors may take an elevator or an iron stairway to the top. The first elevator was a steam hoist. It was replaced in 1901 by an electric elevator. The elevator used today was installed in 1959 and takes seventy seconds to reach the top. The stairway has 897 steps and fifty landings. One hundred eighty-eight carved stones presented by individuals, societies, cities, states, and foreign countries help make up the interior wall.

The monument is 555 feet 5⅛ inches tall, making it the tallest masonry structure in the world, and weighs 90,854 tons. The width at the base of the shaft is 55 feet 1½ inches, the width at the top is 34 feet 5½ inches. In a 30-mile-per-hour wind, the monument sways 0.125 of an inch.

The monument is open from 9:00 a.m. to 5:00 p.m., the day after Labor Day to March 31, and from 8:00 a.m. to midnight, April 1 to Labor Day. The building is closed on Christmas.

Admission is free, and the monument is handicapped accessible.

Washington National Cathedral

The last piece of the fourteenth-century Gothic-style Washington National Cathedral will be fit into place September 29, 1990, eighty-three years to the day the cornerstone was laid by President Theodore Roosevelt.

Sitting atop Mount St. Alban, at Massachusetts and Wisconsin avenues, NW, the completed cathedral will be 514 feet long, 135 feet wide at the nave, and 150 feet high at the roof ridge. It is the sixth largest in the world and the second largest in the United States.

The architects who worked on the Episcopal church were George Frederick Bodley, Henry Vaughan, Philip Hubert

Frohman, E. Donald Robb, Henry B. Little, Anthony J. Segreti, and Robert C. Smith.

The cathedral visiting hours are 10:00 a.m. to 4:30 p.m. daily. Tours are given from 10:00 a.m. to 3:15 p.m. Monday through Saturday and from 12:30 p.m. to 2:45 p.m. on Sunday, except during services. The Pilgrim Observatory Gallery offers a magnificent view of Washington.

The cathedral is handicapped accessible.

Appendix

Capitol Hill

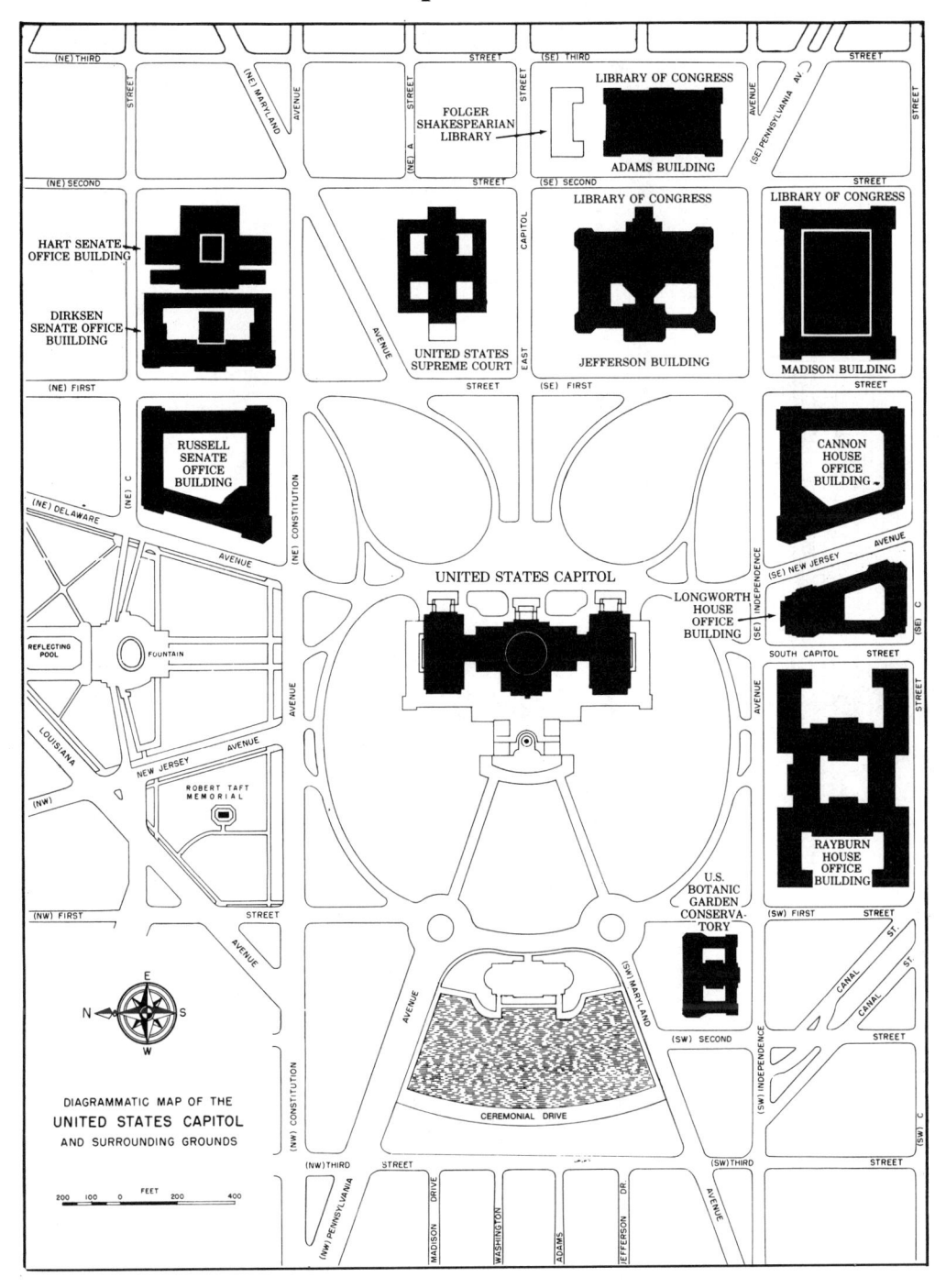

163

Capitol Floor Plan

West Front

East Front

First (Ground) Floor

Scale: 0 16 32 48 64 Feet

H 102, 104-105, 111-112, 151 Clerk of the House
H 106-107, 107A, 108-110, 114 Majority Leader
H 117-121 House Restaurant
H 124-125, 129 Sergeant-at-Arms
H 126 Parliamentarian
H 132-134 Majority Whip
H 136-137 Ways and Means Committee
H 139 Foreign Affairs Committee
H 140 Appropriations Committee
H 153-156 Doorkeeper of the House
S 109-115 Senate Restaurant
S 116-117 Foreign Relations Committee
S 118-119, 121 Democratic Policy Committee
S 125-131, 146 Appropriations Committee
S 132-133 Parliamentarian
S 141 Old Supreme Court Chamber
S 148-150 Democratic Whip
EF 100 Reception room

Capitol Floor Plan

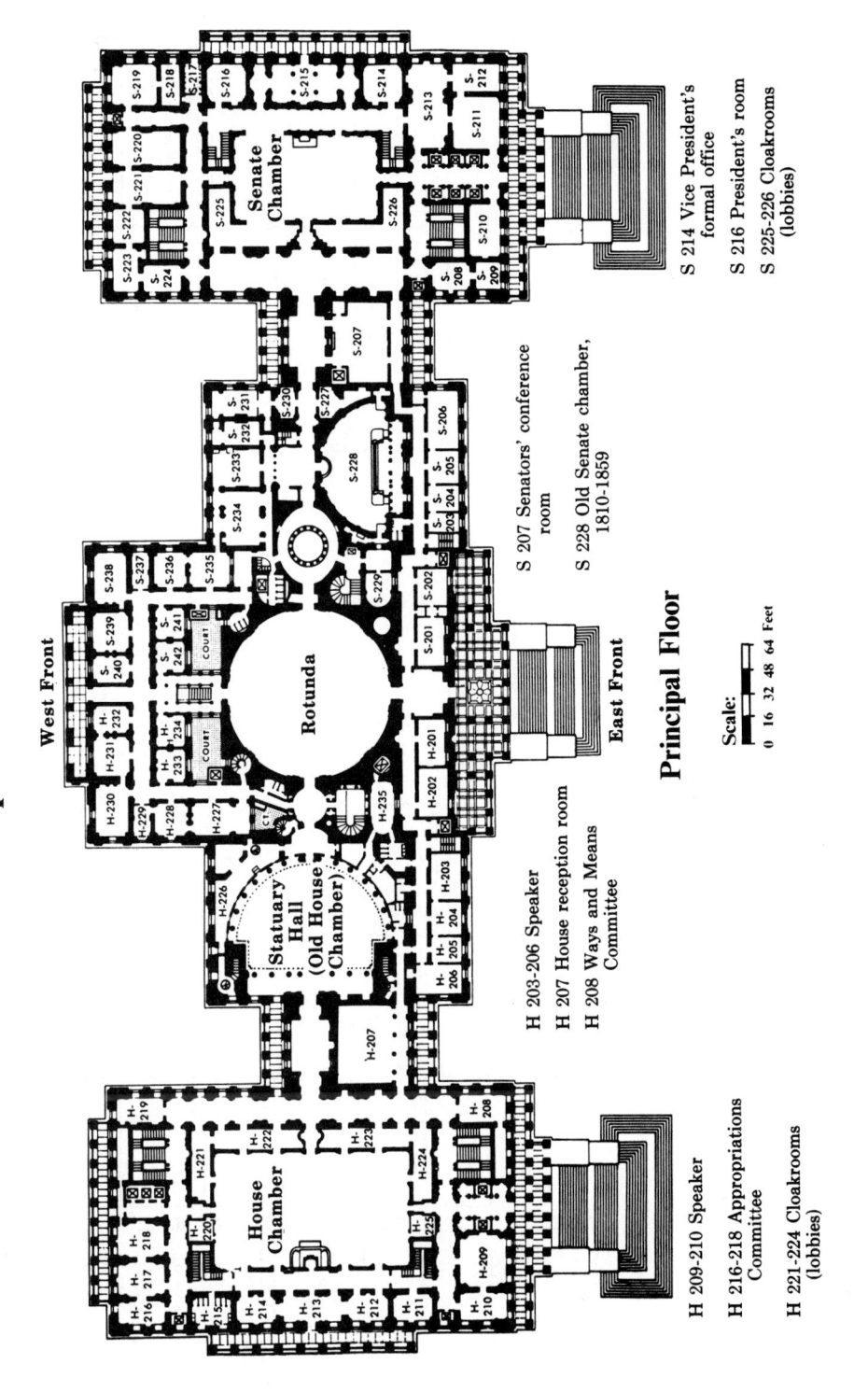

West Front

Rotunda

Statuary Hall (Old House Chamber)

Senate Chamber

House Chamber

East Front

Principal Floor

Scale: 0 16 32 48 64 Feet

S 207 Senators' conference room
S 228 Old Senate chamber, 1810-1859

S 214 Vice President's formal office
S 216 President's room
S 225-226 Cloakrooms (lobbies)

H 203-206 Speaker
H 207 House reception room
H 208 Ways and Means Committee

H 209-210 Speaker
H 216-218 Appropriations Committee
H 221-224 Cloakrooms (lobbies)

U.S. Senate

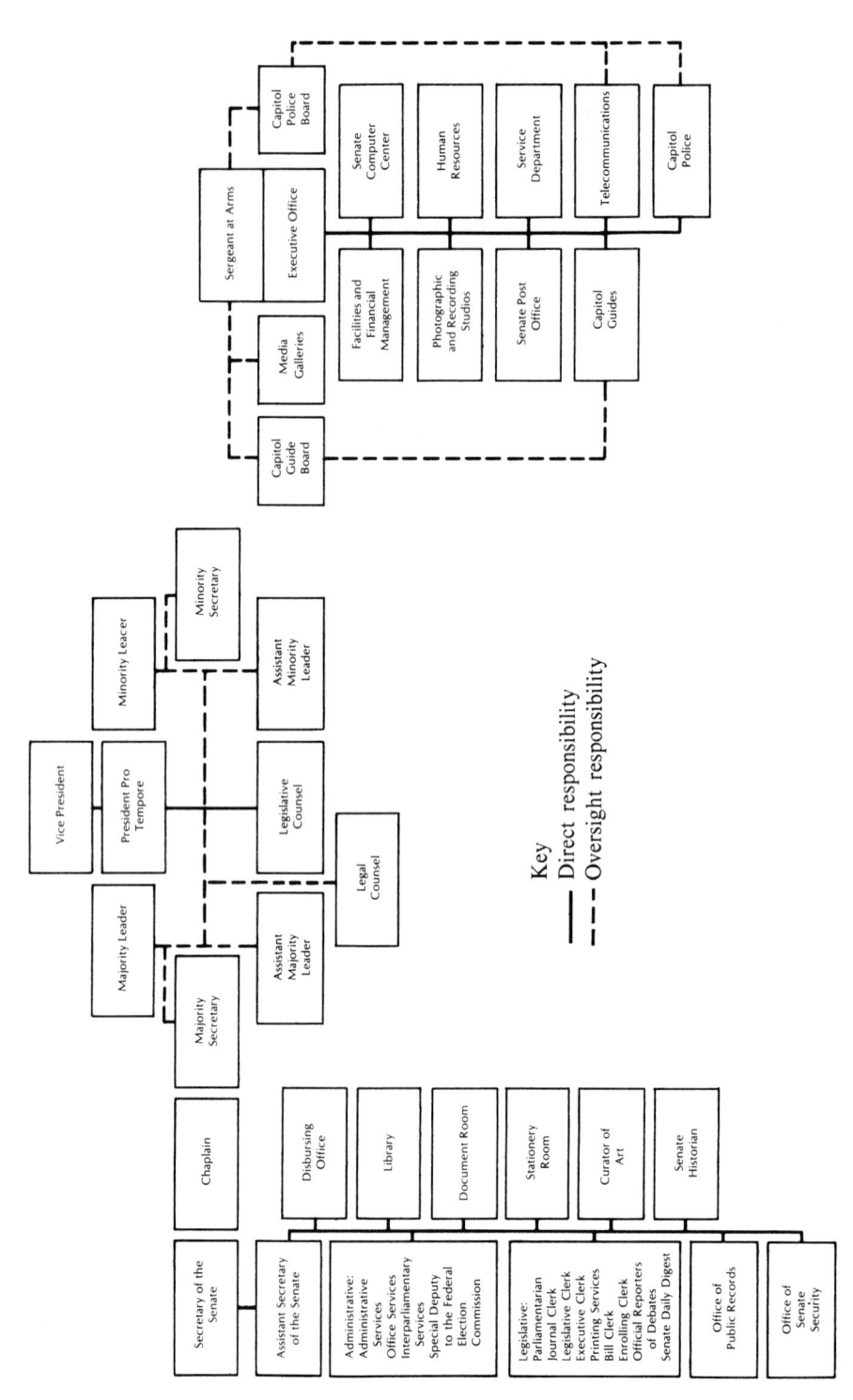

Key
— Direct responsibility
--- Oversight responsibility

Leadership

- Vice President
- President Pro Tempore
- Majority Leader
- Minority Leader
- Assistant Majority Leader
- Assistant Minority Leader
- Majority Secretary
- Minority Secretary
- Legislative Counsel
- Legal Counsel

Secretary of the Senate

- Chaplain
- Assistant Secretary of the Senate
  - Disbursing Office
  - Library
  - Document Room
  - Stationery Room
  - Curator of Art
  - Senate Historian
- Administrative:
  - Administrative Services
  - Office Services
  - Interparliamentary Services
  - Special Deputy to the Federal Election Commission
- Legislative:
  - Parliamentarian
  - Journal Clerk
  - Legislative Clerk
  - Executive Clerk
  - Printing Services
  - Bill Clerk
  - Enrolling Clerk
  - Official Reporters of Debates
  - Senate Daily Digest
- Office of Public Records
- Office of Senate Security

Sergeant at Arms

- Capitol Guide Board
- Media Galleries
- Executive Office
- Capitol Police Board
  - Senate Computer Center
  - Human Resources
  - Service Department
  - Telecommunications
  - Capitol Police
  - Facilities and Financial Management
  - Photographic and Recording Studios
  - Senate Post Office
  - Capitol Guides

Plan of Senate Chamber

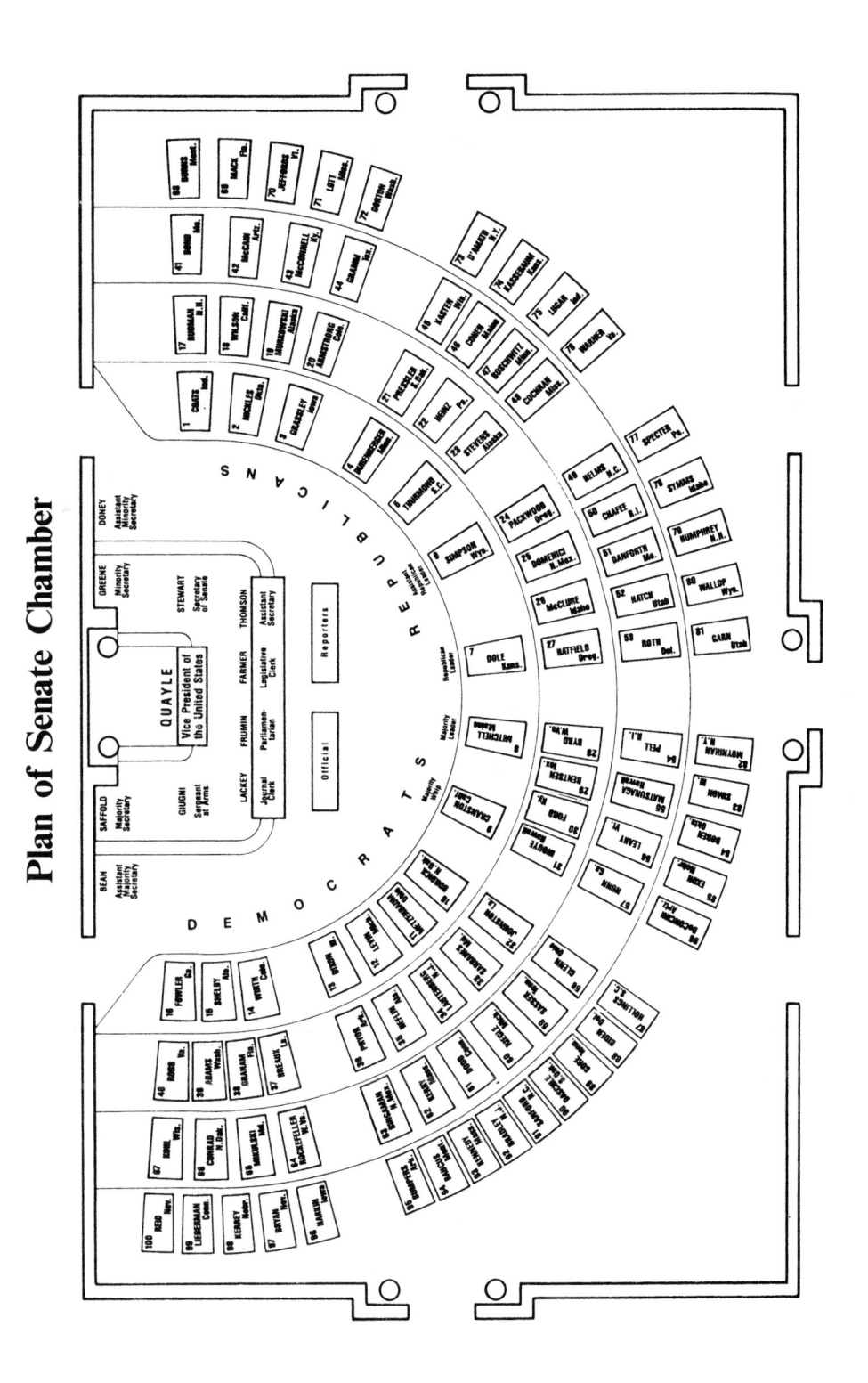

U.S. House of Representatives

- House of Representatives
  - Majority Leader
    - Majority Whip
  - Minority Leader
    - Minority Whip
  - The Speaker
    - Parliamentarian
      - Law Revision Counsel
    - Clerk
    - Doorkeeper
      - Sergeant at Arms
      - Chaplain
      - Postmaster
    - Committee on Rules
      - Legislative Counsel
      - House Office Buildings Commission

Plan of House Chamber

How a Bill Becomes Law

This graphic shows the most typical way in which proposed legislation is enacted into law. There are more complicated, as well as simpler, routes, and most bills fall by the wayside and never become law.

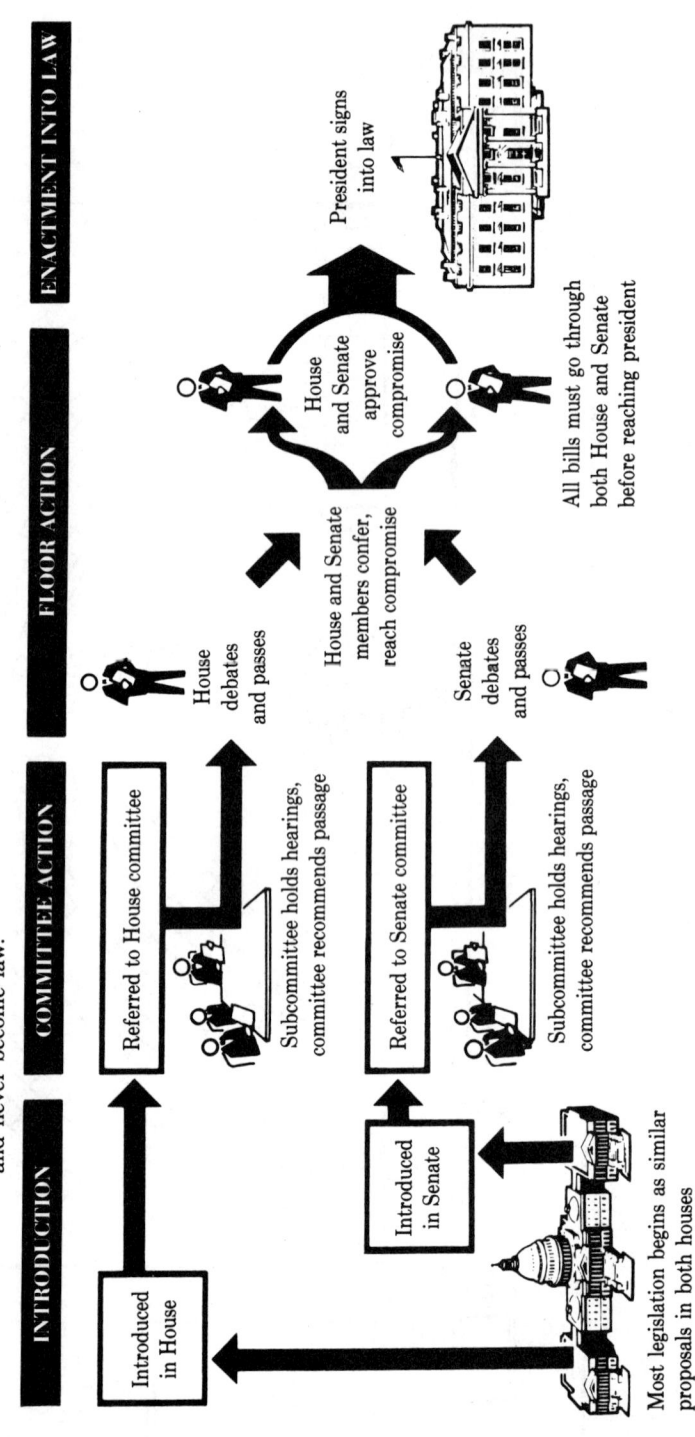

INTRODUCTION

Introduced in House

Introduced in Senate

Most legislation begins as similar proposals in both houses

COMMITTEE ACTION

Referred to House committee

Subcommittee holds hearings, committee recommends passage

Referred to Senate committee

Subcommittee holds hearings, committee recommends passage

FLOOR ACTION

House debates and passes

Senate debates and passes

House and Senate members confer, reach compromise

House and Senate approve compromise

All bills must go through both House and Senate before reaching president

ENACTMENT INTO LAW

President signs into law

Writing Your Member of Congress

If you're writing your member of Congress to request White House tour tickets or passes to the House and Senate visitors' galleries, the forms of address shown below should be used. You may also find the information helpful if you have a complaint, suggestion, or comment you want to make to Congress or the executive branch.

Writing Tips

The following hints on how to write a member of Congress were suggested by congressional sources and the League of Women Voters:

- Write to your own senators or representative. Letters sent to other members will end up on the desk of members from your state.
- Write at the proper time, when a bill is being discussed in committee or on the floor.
- Use your own words and your own stationery. Avoid signing and sending a form or mimeographed letter.
- Don't be a pen pal. Don't try to instruct the representative or senator on every issue that comes up.
- Don't demand a commitment before all the facts are in. Bills rarely become law in the same form as introduced.
- Whenever possible, identify all bills by their number.
- If possible, include pertinent editorials from local papers.
- Be constructive. If a bill deals with a problem you admit exists but you believe the bill is the wrong approach, tell what you think the right approach is.
- If you have expert knowledge or wide experience in particular areas, share it with the member. But don't pretend to wield vast political influence.
- Write to the member when he does something you approve of. A note of appreciation will make him remember you more favorably the next time.
- Feel free to write when you have a question or problem dealing with procedures of government departments.
- Be brief, write legibly, and be sure to use the proper form of address. Feminine forms of address should be substituted as appropriate.

Appendix

President

    The President
    The White House
    Washington, D.C. 20500

    Dear Mr. President:

    Very respectfully yours,

Vice President

    The Vice President
    Old Executive Office Building
    Seventeenth Street and Pennsylvania Avenue, NW
    Washington, D.C. 20510

    Dear Mr. Vice President:

    Sincerely yours,

Senator

    Honorable _____
    United States Senate
    Washington, D.C. 20510

    Dear Senator _____

    Sincerely yours,

Representative

    Honorable _____
    House of Representatives
    Washington, D.C. 20515

    Dear Mr. _____

    Sincerely yours,

Member of the Cabinet

    Honorable _____
    The Secretary of _____
    Washington, D.C. 20520

    Dear Mr. Secretary:

    Sincerely yours,

Plan of the White House

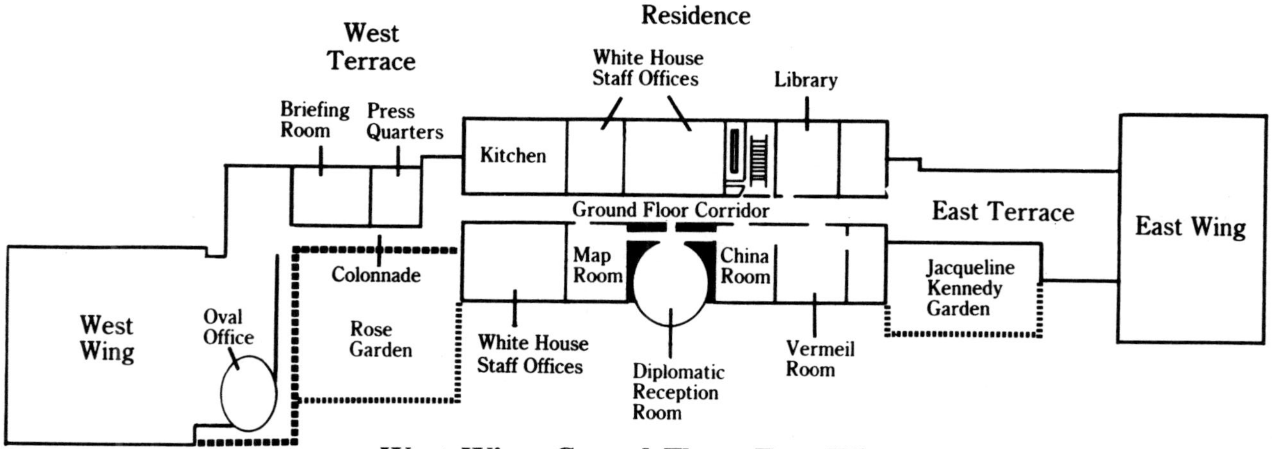

Residence

- White House Staff Offices
- Library
- Kitchen
- Ground Floor Corridor
- China Room
- Map Room
- Vermeil Room
- Diplomatic Reception Room
- White House Staff Offices
- East Terrace
- Jacqueline Kennedy Garden
- East Wing

West Wing, Ground Floor, East Wing

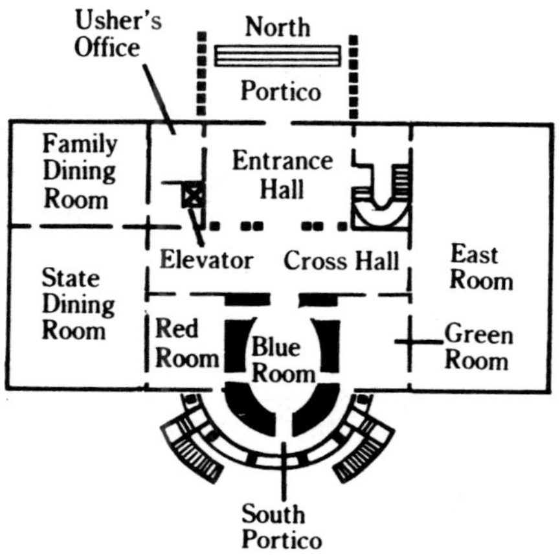

- West Terrace
- Briefing Room
- Press Quarters
- Colonnade
- Rose Garden
- Oval Office
- West Wing

Second Floor

- Queen's Sitting Room
- Queen's Bedroom
- Bedrooms
- President's Dining Room
- Kitchen
- East Sitting Hall
- Center Hall
- Elevator
- West Sitting Hall
- Lincoln Sitting Room
- Lincoln Bedroom
- Treaty Room
- Truman Balcony
- Yellow Oval Room
- President's Study
- President's Bedroom
- Dressing Room

First, or State, Floor

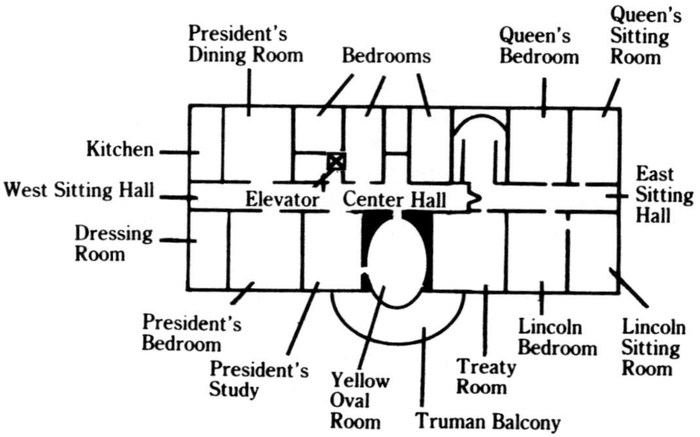

- North Portico
- Entrance Hall
- Cross Hall
- East Room
- Green Room
- Blue Room
- Red Room
- South Portico
- Elevator
- Usher's Office
- Family Dining Room
- State Dining Room

Note: Drawings are not to scale.

U.S. Presidents and Vice Presidents

President and political party	Born	Died	Age at inauguration	Native of	Elected from	Term of service	Vice president
George Washington (F)	1732	1799	57	Va.	Va.	April 30, 1789-March 4, 1793	John Adams
George Washington (F)			61			March 4, 1793-March 4, 1797	John Adams
John Adams (F)	1735	1826	61	Mass.	Mass.	March 4, 1797-March 4, 1801	Thomas Jefferson
Thomas Jefferson (DR)	1743	1826	57	Va.	Va.	March 4, 1801-March 4, 1805	Aaron Burr
Thomas Jefferson (DR)			61			March 4, 1805-March 4, 1809	George Clinton
James Madison (DR)	1751	1836	57	Va.	Va.	March 4, 1809-March 4, 1813	George Clinton
James Madison (DR)			61			March 4, 1813-March 4, 1817	Elbridge Gerry
James Monroe (DR)	1758	1831	58	Va.	Va.	March 4, 1817-March 4, 1821	Daniel D. Tompkins
James Monroe (DR)			62			March 4, 1821-March 4, 1825	Daniel D. Tompkins
John Q. Adams (DR)	1767	1848	57	Mass.	Mass.	March 4, 1825-March 4, 1829	John C. Calhoun
Andrew Jackson (D)	1767	1845	61	S.C.	Tenn.	March 4, 1829-March 4, 1833	John C. Calhoun
Andrew Jackson (D)			65			March 4, 1833-March 4, 1837	Martin Van Buren
Martin Van Buren (D)	1782	1862	54	N.Y.	N.Y.	March 4, 1837-March 4, 1841	Richard M. Johnson
W. H. Harrison (W)	1773	1841	68	Va.	Ohio	March 4, 1841-April 4, 1841	John Tyler
John Tyler (W)	1790	1862	51	Va.	Va.	April 6, 1841-March 4, 1845	
James K. Polk (D)	1795	1849	49	N.C.	Tenn.	March 4, 1845-March 4, 1849	George M. Dallas
Zachary Taylor (W)	1784	1850	64	Va.	La.	March 4, 1849-July 9, 1850	Millard Fillmore
Millard Fillmore (W)	1800	1874	50	N.Y.	N.Y.	July 10, 1850-March 4, 1853	
Franklin Pierce (D)	1804	1869	48	N.H.	N.H.	March 4, 1853-March 4, 1857	William R. King
James Buchanan (D)	1791	1868	65	Pa.	Pa.	March 4, 1857-March 4, 1861	John C. Breckinridge
Abraham Lincoln (R)	1809	1865	52	Ky.	Ill.	March 4, 1861-March 4, 1865	Hannibal Hamlin
Abraham Lincoln (R)			56			March 4, 1865-April 15, 1865	Andrew Johnson
Andrew Johnson (R)	1808	1875	56	N.C.	Tenn.	April 15, 1865-March 4, 1869	
Ulysses S. Grant (R)	1822	1885	46	Ohio	Ill.	March 4, 1869-March 4, 1873	Schuyler Colfax
Ulysses S. Grant (R)			50			March 4, 1873-March 4, 1877	Henry Wilson
Rutherford B. Hayes (R)	1822	1893	54	Ohio	Ohio	March 4, 1877-March 4, 1881	William A. Wheeler
James A. Garfield (R)	1831	1881	49	Ohio	Ohio	March 4, 1881-Sept. 19, 1881	Chester A. Arthur
Chester A. Arthur (R)	1830	1886	50	Vt.	N.Y.	Sept. 20, 1881-March 4, 1885	
Grover Cleveland (D)	1837	1908	47	N.J.	N.Y.	March 4, 1885-March 4, 1889	Thomas A. Hendricks
Benjamin Harrison (R)	1833	1901	55	Ohio	Ind.	March 4, 1889-March 4, 1893	Levi P. Morton

Grover Cleveland (D)	1837	1908	55	Ohio	March 4, 1893-March 4, 1897	Adlai E. Stevenson
William McKinley (R)	1843	1901	54	Ohio	March 4, 1897-March 4, 1901	Garret A. Hobart
William McKinley (R)			58	Ohio	March 4, 1901-Sept. 14, 1901	Theodore Roosevelt
Theodore Roosevelt (R)	1858	1919	42	N.Y.	Sept. 14, 1901-March 4, 1905	
Theodore Roosevelt (R)			46	N.Y.	March 4, 1905-March 4, 1909	Charles W. Fairbanks
William H. Taft (R)	1857	1930	51	Ohio	March 4, 1909-March 4, 1913	James S. Sherman
Woodrow Wilson (D)	1856	1924	56	Va.	March 4, 1913-March 4, 1917	Thomas R. Marshall
Woodrow Wilson (D)			60		March 4, 1917-March 4, 1921	Thomas R. Marshall
Warren G. Harding (R)	1865	1923	55	Ohio	March 4, 1921-Aug. 2, 1923	Calvin Coolidge
Calvin Coolidge (R)	1872	1933	51	Vt.	Aug. 3, 1923-March 4, 1925	
Calvin Coolidge (R)			52		March 4, 1925-March 4, 1929	Charles G. Dawes
Herbert Hoover (R)	1874	1964	54	Iowa	March 4, 1929-March 4, 1933	Charles Curtis
Franklin D. Roosevelt (D)	1882	1945	51	N.Y.	March 4, 1933-Jan. 20, 1937	John N. Garner
Franklin D. Roosevelt (D)			55		Jan. 20, 1937-Jan. 20, 1941	John N. Garner
Franklin D. Roosevelt (D)			59		Jan. 20, 1941-Jan. 20, 1945	Henry A. Wallace
Franklin D. Roosevelt (D)			63		Jan. 20, 1945-April 12, 1945	Harry S Truman
Harry S Truman (D)	1884	1972	60	Mo.	April 12, 1945-Jan. 20, 1949	
Harry S Truman (D)			64		Jan. 20, 1949-Jan. 20, 1953	Alben W. Barkley
Dwight D. Eisenhower (R)	1890	1969	62	Texas	Jan. 20, 1953-Jan. 20, 1957	Richard Nixon
Dwight D. Eisenhower (R)			66	Pa.	Jan. 20, 1957-Jan. 20, 1961	Richard Nixon
John F. Kennedy (D)	1917	1963	43	Mass.	Jan. 20, 1961-Nov. 22, 1963	Lyndon B. Johnson
Lyndon B. Johnson (D)	1908	1973	55	Texas	Nov. 22, 1963-Jan. 20, 1965	
Lyndon B. Johnson (D)			56		Jan. 20, 1965-Jan. 20, 1969	Hubert H. Humphrey
Richard Nixon (R)	1913		56	N.Y.	Jan. 20, 1969-Jan. 20, 1973	Spiro T. Agnew
Richard Nixon (R)			60	Calif.	Jan. 20, 1973-Aug. 9, 1974	Spiro T. Agnew Gerald R. Ford
Gerald R. Ford (R)	1913		61	Neb.	Aug. 9, 1974-Jan. 20, 1977	Nelson A. Rockefeller
Jimmy Carter (D)	1924		52	Ga.	Jan. 20, 1977-Jan. 20, 1981	Walter F. Mondale
Ronald Reagan (R)	1911		69	Ill.	Jan. 20, 1981-Jan. 20, 1985	George Bush
Ronald Reagan (R)			73		Jan. 20, 1985-Jan. 20, 1989	George Bush
George Bush (R)	1924		64	Mass. Texas	Jan. 20, 1989-	Dan Quayle

Note: D—Democrat; DR—Democratic-Republican; F—Federalist; R—Republican; W—Whig.

Glossary of Congressional Terms

Act—The term for legislation once it has passed both houses of Congress and has been signed by the president or passed over his veto, thus becoming law.

Amendment—A proposal to alter the language or provisions in a bill or in another amendment.

Amendment in the Nature of a Substitute—An amendment that seeks to replace the entire text of a bill or replaces a large portion of it.

Appropriations Bill—A bill that gives legal authority to spend or obligate money from the Treasury. An appropriations bill generally cannot provide more money than has been authorized for a particular program under separate legislation.

Authorization—Basic, substantive legislation that establishes or continues the legal operation of a federal program or agency, either indefinitely or for a specific period of time. An authorization normally is a prerequisite for an appropriation and sets a ceiling for it.

Bills—Most legislative proposals before Congress are in the form of bills and are designated by HR in the House of Representatives or S in the Senate, according to the house in which they originate, and by a number assigned in the order in which they are introduced during the two-year period of a Congress. "Public bills" deal with general questions and become public laws if approved by Congress and signed by the president. "Private bills" deal with such matters as an individual's claim against the government or special immigration request, and become private laws if approved and signed.

Bills Introduced—Any number of members may join in introducing a bill or resolution. The first member listed is the sponsor of the bill; the others are cosponsors.

Bills Referred—When introduced, a bill is referred to the committee or committees that have jurisdiction over the subject of the bill.

Budget—The document sent to Congress by the president early each year estimating government revenue and expenditures for the ensuing fiscal year.

Budget Resolution—A concurrent resolution passed by both houses of Congress, but not requiring the president's signature,

Appendix

setting forth or revising the congressional budget for the following three fiscal years.

By Request—A phrase used when a member introduces a bill at the request of an executive agency or private organization but does not necessarily endorse it.

Calendar—An agenda of business awaiting possible action by the chamber. The House uses five legislative calendars—the Consent, Discharge, House, Private, and Union calendars, according to the type of bill involved. The Senate uses only an executive calendar.

Clean Bill—Frequently after a committee has finished a major revision of a bill, one of the committee members will assemble the changes and what is left of the original bill into a new measure and introduce it as a "clean bill." The revised measure, which is given a new number, then is referred back to the committee, which reports it to the floor for consideration.

Clerk of the House—Chief administrative officer of the House of Representatives.

Cloture—The process in the Senate for ending a filibuster other than by unanimous consent. A petition to limit debate must be signed by sixteen senators, and the motion to invoke cloture then must be agreed to by three-fifths of the Senate's membership.

Committee—A division of the House or Senate that prepares legislation for action by the parent chamber or makes investigations as directed by the parent chamber. Most committees are divided into subcommittees, which study legislation, hold hearings, and report bills to the full committee.

Committee of the Whole—The working title of what is formally "The Committee of the Whole House on the State of the Union." To expedite business, the House resolves itself into the Committee of the Whole to consider amendments to most major bills. The Speaker is supplanted with a "chairman" who presides over debate and voting on amendments. When work on a measure is complete, the Committee "rises," the Speaker returns to the chair, and the full House then votes on passage of the legislation.

Concurrent Resolution—A statement expressing the sense of Congress on some issue. Designated H Con Res or S Con Res, depending on the chamber of origin, it must be adopted by both houses, but it does not go to the president or have the force of law.

Conference—A meeting between selected members of the House and Senate to reconcile differences between the two chambers' versions of the same legislation.

Appendix

Congressional Record—The daily, printed account of proceedings in the House and Senate, with a substantially verbatim account of debate. Members are allowed to revise their spoken remarks.

Continuing Resolution—A joint resolution to continue appropriations for a department or agency when a fiscal year is beginning and Congress has not enacted the department's regular appropriations bill. Also called "CR" or continuing appropriations.

Division Vote—A vote in which all members present who favor a bill are asked to stand, followed by all those opposed. No record is kept of how members voted (also called "standing vote").

Entitlement Program—A federal program such as Social Security or unemployment compensation that guarantees a certain level of benefits to persons who meet requirements set by law.

Filibuster—A time-delaying strategy of debate, quorum calls, amendments, and other procedures used by a minority to defeat or achieve compromise on a proposition favored by the majority.

Fiscal Year—Financial operations of the government are carried out in a twelve-month period beginning October 1 each year. Fiscal 1990, for example, began October 1, 1989, and will end September 30, 1990.

Five-Minute Rule—A debate-limiting rule of the House that, while the Committee of the Whole sits, allows a member offering an amendment to speak for five minutes in its favor, followed by an opponent who also speaks for five minutes.

Floor Manager—A member who has the task of steering legislation through floor debate and the amending process to a final vote in the chamber. Usually the chairman or ranking minority member of the committee that reported the legislation.

Frank—A member's facsimile signature, which is used on envelopes in lieu of stamps, for the member's official outgoing mail. The "franking privilege" is the right to send mail postage-free.

Germane—Pertaining to the subject matter of the measure at hand.

Gramm-Rudman-Hollings Deficit Reduction Act—Legislation to balance the federal budget by fiscal year 1993. The law established annual maximum deficit targets and mandated across-the-board automatic cuts ("sequestration") in most federal programs if the deficit goals were not achieved through

Appendix

regular budget actions.

Hearings—Committee sessions for taking testimony from witnesses. The public and press may attend open hearings; the vast majority of hearings are open to the public.

Hopper—Box on House clerk's desk where members deposit bills and resolutions to be introduced.

Joint Resolution—A resolution requiring approval of both the House and Senate. It becomes law if signed by the president or passed over his veto. Differing in no substantive way from a bill, a joint resolution often is used to address a limited matter. A joint resolution also is used for a constitutional amendment, which requires passage by two-thirds of each chamber but does not go to the president.

Law—An act of Congress that has been signed by the president or passed over his veto by Congress. Public bills, when signed, become public laws and are cited by the letters PL and a hyphenated number.

Majority Leader—In the Senate, the majority leader, in consultation with the minority leader, directs the legislative schedule for the chamber. He also is his party's spokesperson and chief strategist. In the House, the majority leader is second to the Speaker and serves as his party's legislative strategist. There also is a minority leader, who is the floor leader for the minority party in each chamber.

Majority Whip—In effect, the assistant majority leader, in either the House or Senate. His job is to help marshal majority forces in support of party strategy and legislation. There also is a minority whip, who performs duties of whip for the minority party.

Marking Up a Bill—Working on legislation in committee or subcommittee, approving, amending, or rejecting each provision and the bill as a whole.

Morning Hour—Time set aside for the conduct of routine business. The House rarely has a morning hour.

Motion—A request by a member to institute any one of a wide array of parliamentary actions. He "moves" for a certain procedure, such as the consideration of a measure.

Nominations—Presidential appointments to government and diplomatic posts that are subject to Senate confirmation.

One-Minute Speeches—Delivered at the beginning of a legislative day in the House, these may cover any topic but are limited to one minute in duration.

Override a Veto—If the president disapproves a bill and sends it back to Congress with his objections, Congress may try to override his veto and enact the bill into law. The override

Appendix

requires a recorded vote with a two-thirds majority in each chamber.

Pair—A "gentleman's agreement" between two lawmakers who are on opposite sides of an issue, made in advance of a vote to cancel out the effects of absences. Notices of pairs are printed in the *Congressional Record.*

Parliamentarian—Each chamber employs several parliamentarians to assist the presiding officer in making rulings and conducting business of the chamber.

Pocket Veto—The act of the president in withholding his approval of a bill after Congress has adjourned.

Point of Order—An objection raised by a member that the chamber is departing from rules governing its conduct of business. The chair then must rule on whether the objection is justified.

President of the Senate—The vice president of the United States presides over the Senate. In his absence, a president pro tempore presides.

President Pro Tempore—The presiding officer of the Senate in the absence of the vice president of the United States.

Previous Question—A motion that, if approved, has the effect of cutting off all debate, preventing further amendments, and forcing a vote on the pending matter.

Quorum—The number of members whose presence is necessary for transaction of business. In the Senate, a majority of the membership comprises a quorum. In the House, a quorum also is a majority of the members, except in the Committee of the Whole House, where it is one hundred members.

Readings of Bills—Traditionally, a bill has to be read three times before passage. In modern practice, a bill is considered to have been read first upon introduction, second upon floor consideration, and third after all floor debate. Seldom are bills actually read aloud in their entirety.

Recommit to Committee—A motion made after a bill has been debated to return it to the committee that reported it. Recommittal usually is a death blow to a bill, unless done with instructions to adopt a particular amendment and report the bill back to the chamber.

Reconciliation—The 1974 budget act provides for a "reconciliation" procedure for bringing tax and appropriations bills into conformity with congressional budget resolutions. Congress instructs its legislative committees to approve measures adjusting revenues and expenditures by a certain amount by a given deadline. The recommendations of these committees are consolidated without change by the Budget committees into an

Appendix

omnibus reconciliation bill, which then must be approved by both houses of Congress.

Reconsider a Vote—A motion to reconsider the vote by which an action was taken has the effect, until disposed of, of putting the action in abeyance. Such a motion can be made only by a member who voted on the prevailing side.

Recorded Vote—A vote on which a public record is kept of each member's stand. In the Senate, this is accomplished through a roll call of the senators. The House uses an electronic voting system, and a recorded vote can be obtained on demand of one-fifth of a quorum (forty-four members) of the full house, or one-fourth (twenty-five) during Committee of the Whole.

Report—Both a verb and a noun as a congressional term. After completing a markup of a bill, a committee reports its recommendations to the chamber along with the measure. It usually publishes a written report containing an explanation of the bill as approved and the committee's reasons for its action.

Resolution—Designated H Res or S Res, a "simple" resolution deals with matters entirely within the prerogatives of one house. It does not require passage by the other chamber or approval by the president, and it does not have the force of law.

Rider—An amendment, usually not germane, that a sponsor offers to a bill to enhance the amendment's chances of enactment.

Rules—The term has two congressional meanings. Both houses of Congress have standing rules governing procedure. In the House, the term also refers to resolutions reported by the Rules Committee, which, upon approval by the full House, govern the length and terms of debate for most bills considered on the floor.

Secretary of the Senate—The chief administrative officer of the Senate.

Speaker—The presiding officer of the House of Representatives.

Strike Out the Last Word—In the House's Committee of the Whole, when debate is limited by the five-minute rule, a member may gain recognition from the chair by moving to "strike out the last word" of the amendment or section of a bill under consideration. The motion is pro forma, requires no vote, and does not alter the measure being debated. Members also use "strike out the requisite number of words."

Supplemental Appropriations Bill—Legislation appropriating added funds for a department during the current fiscal year after its regular appropriations bill has been enacted.

Appendix

Suspend the Rules—A time-saving procedure used for considering bills in the House under which no amendments may be offered and debate is limited to twenty minutes per side. A two-thirds vote is required for passage under suspension of the rules, a procedure reserved mostly for noncontroversial bills.

Table a Bill—A motion to "lay on the table" effectively kills a bill if approved.

Treaties—Executive proposals, such as arms control proposals, that must be submitted to the Senate for approval by two-thirds of the senators present.

Unanimous Consent—The Senate or House can do almost anything it wishes, regardless of its rules, upon unanimous consent of the chamber. But objection from a single member can block action.

Unanimous Consent Agreement—Also called a time limitation agreement, it is an agreement negotiated by the Senate leadership to govern one or more aspects of action on a measure. In effect, it is similar to a rule in the House.

Veto—Disapproval by the president of a bill or joint resolution. When Congress is in session, the president must veto a bill within ten days, excluding Sundays, after he has received it; otherwise, it becomes law without his signature.

Voice Vote—Members answer "aye" or "no" in chorus, and the presiding officer decides the result. No record is made of how individual members voted.

Yeas and Nays—A recorded vote (see above).

Yield—When a member has been recognized to speak, no other member may speak unless he obtains permission from the member recognized. Requests are made in the form, "Will the gentleman yield?"

Additional Reading

Applewhite, E. J. *Washington Itself: An Informal Guide to the Capital of the United States.* New York: Knopf, 1989.

Benjaminson, Margaret Seawell, "Housing of the Executive Branch," in *Guide to the Presidency,* ed. Michael Nelson. Washington, D.C.: Congressional Quarterly, 1989.

Congress A to Z: CQ's Ready Reference Encyclopedia. Washington, D.C.: Congressional Quarterly, 1988.

Congressional Directory, 1989-1990, One Hundred First Congress. Washington, D.C.: Government Printing Office, 1989.

Executive Office of the President, Office of Administration. *The Old Executive Office Building: A Victorian Masterpiece.* Washington, D.C.: Government Printing Office, 1984.

Guide to Congress. 3d. ed. Washington, D.C.: Congressional Quarterly, 1982.

Jensen, Amy La Follette. *The White House and Its Thirty-three Families.* New York: McGraw-Hill, 1962.

Leish, Kenneth W. *The White House.* New York: Newsweek, 1972.

The Living White House. 7th rev. ed. Washington, D.C.: White House Historical Association, 1982.

Look, David W., and Carole L. Perrault. *The Interior Building and Its Architecture and Its Art.* Washington, D.C.: Government Printing Office, 1986.

Oulahan, Richard. "Capital's Doughty Dowager Becomes a New Cinderella." *Smithsonian.* March 1986. 84-94.

Price, Robert L., ed. *The Washington Post Guide to Washington.* 2d. ed. New York: McGraw-Hill, 1989.

Seale, William. *The President's House.* 2 vols. Washington, D.C.: White House Historical Association, 1986.

Vasaio, Antonio, and the Justice Management Division. *The Fiftieth Anniversary of the U.S. Department of Justice Building, 1934-1984.* Washington, D.C.: Government Printing Office, 1984.

Washington Past and Present: A Guide to the Nation's Capital. 2d. ed. Washington, D.C.: United States Capitol Historical Society, 1987.

Appendix

We, the People: The Story of the United States Capitol, Its Past and Its Promise. Washington, D.C.: United States Capitol Historical Society, 1985.

West, J. B., with Mary Lynn Kotz. *Upstairs at the White House: My Life with the First Ladies.* New York: Coward, McCann, and Geoghegan, 1973.

The White House: An Historic Guide. 16th ed. Washington, D.C.: White House Historical Association, 1987.

Witt, Elder. *Guide to the U.S. Supreme Court.* 2d. ed. Washington, D.C.: Congressional Quarterly, 1989.

Index

Index

Adams, Abigail, 85-86, 93
Adams, John, 13, 22, 62, 139
   White House residence, 85, 94-95, 98
Adams, John Quincy, 22, 25, 94, 103
Adams, William, 32
Adams Building, Library of Congress, 58, 66
Administration, Office of, 110
Administration Building, Agriculture Dept., 117-118
Admiral's House, 113
African marble, 72
Agency for International Development, 126
Agriculture Department, 117-118
Alabama marble, 72
Alexander, Hartley B., 124
Alexander, John W., 58
Alexandria, Va., 5
Algerian marble, 57
Algonquin (pony), 105
Algonquin Indians, 4
Allied Architects, 46
"All in the Family," 147
Amateis, Louis, 30
America (artistic representation), 65
Americana Project, 126
American Booksellers Association, 92
American Film Institute Theatre, Kennedy Center, 139
American Institute of Architects, 24, 60, 123
America's Library, 57
Anacostia Museum, 133
Anthony, Susan B., 30
Apollo 11 Command Module, 141
"Apotheosis of Democracy, The" (Bartlett), 29
"Apotheosis of Washington" (Brumidi), 26
Aquarium, Commerce Dept., 119, 142, 148
Aquia Creek Quarry, 13
Arboretums and gardens
   Botanic Garden, 4, 11, 41-42

Enid A. Haupt Garden, 137-138
Hirshhorn Museum and Sculpture Garden, 138
Jacqueline Kennedy Garden, White House, 90, 104
National Arboretum, 155-156
Poplar Point Nursery, 11, 42
Rose Garden, White House, 104
Architect of the Capitol
   Botanic Garden acting director, 42
   persons holding position, 13, 16, 17, 21, 23-25
Archive of Folk Culture, 63
Archives of American Art, 147, 151
Arlington House, 134
Arlington National Cemetery, 133-134
Armed Forces Institute of Pathology, 150
Arms Control and Disarmament Agency, 126
Army-McCarthy investigation, 36, 51
Army Signal Corps, 108
Art Deco style, 124
Art galleries
   Arthur M. Sackler Gallery, 154
   Corcoran Gallery, 136
   Freer Gallery, 137
   National Gallery, 144-145
   National Museum of African Art, 137, 146
   National Museum of American Art, 146-147, 151
   National Portrait Gallery, 147, 151
   Renwick Gallery, 153-154
Arts and Industries Building, Smithsonian Institution, 134
Augustus, Caesar, 73

Bach manuscripts, 63
Bacon, Francis, 65
Bacon, Henry, 140
Bairstow, Ernest, 140
Baltimore Whig, 97
Barney, Alice Pike, 147
Barney Studio House, 147

Index

Bartholdi, Frederic Auguste, 42
Bartholdi Fountain, 42
Bartlett, Paul Wayland, 29
Bay Psalm Book, 62
Beal, Jack, 125
Beckley, John, 56
Beethoven, Ludwig von, 63, 65
Bell, Alexander Graham, 147
Bellangé, Pierre Antoine, 94
Bell Tavern, 79
Bergstrom, George E., 120
Berks, Robert, 139
Bible collection, 55, 62, 65
Bicentennial (1976), 14, 24, 33, 41, 68, 125
Biddle, George, 125
Biddle, Margaret Thompson, 90
Bierstadt, Albert, 98
Billington, John H., 56, 66
Bill of Rights, 63, 142
Bishop, William W., 56
Blackstone, William, 73
Blashfield, Edwin, 65
Blodget, Samuel, Jr., 16
Blodget's Hotel, 15-16
Blue Room, White House, 92, 94
Bodley, George Frederick, 158
Boehm Quintette, 67
Bonaparte, Napoleon, 73
Boorstin, Daniel J., 56, 66
Booth, John Wilkes, 137
Borglum, Gutzon, 29
Borie, Charles L., Jr., 124
Botanic Garden, 4, 11, 41-42
Bouché, Louis, 123
Bradley, Omar, 134
Brady, Matthew, photographs, 55, 63, 151
Brady, Nicholas F., 53
Brahms manuscripts, 63
Breuer, Marcel, 122, 123
Brick Capitol, 16, 22, 79, 82
Brooks, Barr, Graeber, and White, 125
Brown v. Board of Education, 74
Bruce, Alisa Mellon, 145
Brumidi, Constantino, 26, 28
Brumidi Corridor, Capitol, 28
Buberl, Caspar, 144
Budapest String Quartet, 67
Bulfinch, Charles, 16-17, 43
Bunker, Edith and Archie, chairs, 147
Bunshaft, Gordon, 138
Bureau of Engraving and Printing, 129, 134, 136

Bureau of Labor Statistics, 125
Bureau of Mines, 124
Bureau of War Risk Insurance, 129
Bush, Barbara, 88, 100, 115
Bush, George, 22, 88, 100, 103, 115
Byrd, Richard, 133

Cabinet Room, White House, 102-103
Cafeteria Carousel, National Museum of American History, 149
Cafeterias and restaurants
    Capitol building, 11
    Congressional office buildings, 45
    Library of Congress, 57
    mall-area museums, 148-149
    Old Post Office building, 153
    Supreme Court building, 73
    Union Station, 155
    zoo, 149
Calder, Alexander, 53, 138, 145
Calendar of Events in the Library of Congress, 68
Califano, Joseph A., Jr., 40
"Calling of Cincinnatus from the Plow" (Brumidi), 26
"Calling of Putnam from the Plow to the Revolution" (Brumidi), 26
Cameras permitted. *See* specific buildings and museums
Camp David, 108
Cannon, Joseph G., 46
Cannon House Office Building, 46, 48, 60
Capitol Art Foundation, 53
Capitol building, 9-33, 71
    Centennial Safe, 33
    crypt, 30-31
    dome, 3, 15, 17, 19-20
    doors, 30
    East Front, 16, 21, 23
    1851-1892 expansion, 17-21
    first cornerstone, 12, 123
    flag program, 40-41
    floor plans, 164, 165
    history and description, 3-5, 9-10, 15
    House chamber plan, 169
    House mace, 25, 31-33
    inaugural sites, 4, 9, 22, 23
    landscaping, 20-21
    location, 4-5, 15
    paintings, statues, sculptures, 25-30
    public address system, 19
    Rotunda, 9, 15, 17, 19, 20, 22, 25, 26
    security concerns, 37, 106
    Senate chamber plan, 167

190

Index

1792-1829 construction, 10-17
  subway system, 44, 48-49, 51
  Supreme Court quarters, 76, 78-82
  twentieth-century alterations, 21, 23-25
  visitors information, 11
  West Front, 9, 10, 21, 23-25
Capitol Hill, 3, 163
Capitol Historical Society, 11
Carpenter, Francis B., 25
Carrere and Hastings, 21, 46, 51
Carroll, Daniel, 4, 79
Carter, Jimmy, 98, 100, 101, 125
Casals, Pablo, 94
Cascade Cafe, National Gallery of Art, 149
Casey, Edward Pearce, 56
Casey, Thomas L., 56
Cash Room, Treasury Dept., 129
Cassatt, Mary, 147, 151
Castle, Smithsonian Institution, 154-155
Catlin, George, 147
Caucus Room, Senate, 51
Census clock, 119
Centennial Safe, 33
Center Hall, White House, 98-99
Center Sitting Hall, White House, 101
Central Intelligence Agency, 108
Central Park, N.Y., 20
Cerne Abbey Manor, 4
Certiorari writ, 74-75
Challenger space shuttle, 134
Chandor, Douglas, 90
Charlemagne, 73
Charters of Freedom, 142, 143
Chase, William Merritt, 98
Chatelain, Gauger, and Holan, 121
China Room, White House, 90-91
Christy, Howard Chandler, 91
City Hall, Philadelphia, 77-78
Civil Service Commission, 45
Civil War, 19, 20, 127, 133, 150
Civil War photographs, 55, 63
Clark, Edward, 21
Clerk of the House, 178
Cleveland, Frances Folsom, 94
Cleveland, Grover, 94
Clock tower, Old Post Office building, 153
Coast Guard, 127
Cockburn, George, 14
Cole, Thomas, 147
Colorado, 29
Colorado marble, 140

Columbia Institute for the Promotion of Arts and Sciences, 41
Columbus, Christopher, 30, 65
Comic book collection, 61
Commerce Department, 118-119, 142, 148
Commissioner of public buildings and grounds, 16
Committee. *See* specific committee names
Communication systems, 92, 108
Concert Hall, Kennedy Center, 139
Concourse Buffet, National Gallery of Art, 149
Confucius, 73
Congress Bells, Old Post Office building, 153
Congress Hall, Philadelphia, 22
Congressional activities
  first meeting sites, 4
  glossary of terms, 177-183
  historical practices, 43-44
  House organizational chart, 168
  how bill becomes law, 170
  Library of Congress service, 66
  page program, 37-40
  Senate organizational chart, 166
  TV coverage, 33-37
  typical day, 34-35, 38-39
  writing to members, 171-172
Congressional Globe, 40
Congressional office buildings, 43-53
  features and functions, 44-45
  historical background, 43-44
  House, 45-51
  location, 3
  Senate, 51-53
  subway system, 44, 48-49, 51
  visitors information, 45
Congressional quarters. *See* Capitol building
Congressional Reading Room, Library of Congress, 66
Congressional Record, 40, 179
Congressional Research Service, 60, 66
Consent Calendar, 35
"Constitution, The" (Faulkner), 143
Constitution, U.S., 62, 142
Constitutional Convention notes, 55, 62
Contemporary architectural style, 111, 122
Contemporary Chamber Players of the University of Chicago, 67
Coolidge, Calvin, 103

191

Index

Coolidge, Elizabeth Sprague, Auditorium, Library of Congress, 67
Coolidge, Grace, 91, 101
Copyright law, 56
Copyright Office, 68
Corcoran, William Wilson, 136
Corcoran Gallery of Art, 30, 136, 153
Cornstalk motifs, 25
Costaggini, Filippo, 26
Cotton gin, 147
Council of Economic Advisers, 109
Courtroom, Supreme Court building, 71, 72
Cox, Allyn, 26, 28
Cox, Edward, 104
Crane, Daniel B., 40
Crawford, Thomas, 15, 20, 29, 30
Cross Hall, White House, 92
Crypt, Capitol, 29, 30
Cuban missile crisis, 120
Curry, John Steuart, 125
Curtin Call Cafe, Kennedy Center, 148
Curtis and Davis, 122
Custis, George Washington Parke, 31, 133
Custis, Mary, 133

Dartmouth College v. Woodward, 80
da Vinci, Leonardo, 144
Davis, Jefferson, 18, 20
Declaration of Independence, 55, 62, 138, 142
"Declaration of Independence, The" (Faulkner), 143
Defense Department and Pentagon, 108, 117, 119-122, 123
Degas, Edgar, 138, 151
Deihm, Mrs. Charles F., 33
de Kooning, Willem, 138
Democratic Study Group, 44-45
Departments, 117. *See also* specific department names
Depot of Charts and Instruments, 156
Depression photographs, 63
Dessez, Leon E., 113
Dewitt, Poor, and Shelton, 60
Dickens, Charles, 97-98
Dillon, C. Douglas, 53
Dingell, John D., 40
Diplomatic Lobby, State Dept., 126
Diplomatic Reception Room, White House, 91
Dirksen, Everett McKinley, 51
Dirksen Senate Office Building, 45, 46, 48, 51-52
Discovery Room, Museum of Natural History, 150-151
Discovery Theater, Arts and Industries Building, 134
District of Columbia. *See* Washington, D.C.
Ditchley Foundation, 152
Dole, Robert, 35
Dome, Capitol, 3, 15, 17, 19-20
Donnelly, John, Jr., 72
Draco (lawgiver), 73
Dunlop, John, 62

Earley, John Joseph, 124
East Building, National Gallery of Art, 144-145, 148-149
Easter Monday egg-rolling, 105
East Front, Capitol, 16, 21-23
East Room, White House, 22, 92-94
East Sitting Hall, White House, 96, 99
East Wing, White House, 85, 89, 90
Education Department, 121
Eggers, Otto R., 139
Eggers and Higgins, 51
Egypt, 65
1876 Philadelphia Centennial Exposition, 33, 42, 134
Einstein, Albert, Planetarium, 141
Eisenhower, Dwight D., 22, 23, 31, 103, 110
Eisenhower, Mamie, 100
Eisenhower Theatre, Kennedy Center, 139
Eliot, John, 62
Elisonfon, Eliot, Photographic Archives, 146
Elizabeth II (queen of England), 96
Ellipse, 117
Emancipation Proclamation, 96
Empire State Building, 120
Employment Service, U.S., 45
Encore Cafeteria, Kennedy Center, 148
Energy Department, 122
England, 65
Ernst, Max, 114
Evans, Luther H., 56
Evans, Rudulph, 139
Evans, Walker, 63
Executive Mansion, 97. *See also* White House
Executive office buildings, 109-111
Executive Office of the President, 109-111

192

Index

Exhibition Hall, State Dept., 126
Exhibits Office, Library of Congress, 67
Explorers Hall, National Geographic Society, 145-146

Family Dining Room, White House, 95-96, 99
Farmers Home Administration, 118
Farnsworth, Philo, 29
Faulkner, Barry, 143
Faulkner, Kingsbury, and Stenhouse, 121
Federal Aviation Administration, 127
Federal Bureau of Investigation, 125, 136-137
Federal Energy Regulatory Commission, 122
Federal Hall, New York City, 22
Federal Office Building (FOB) No. 5, 122
Federal Office Building (FOB) No. 6, 121
Federal Triangle, 117, 118, 124
Festival of the Building Arts, 144
Fillmore, Abigail, 98
Fillmore, Millard, 17, 22
Fine Arts Commission, President's, 110, 124-125
Fine Arts Committee, Jacqueline Kennedy's, 100
Fine Arts Committee, State Dept., 126
First ladies
    gowns, 147
    portraits, 90
Flagg, Ernest, 136
Flag program, 40-41
Flight Line Cafeteria, Air and Space Museum, 148
Floor plans and maps
    Capitol building, 164, 165
    Capitol Hill, 163
    House chamber, 169
    Senate chamber, 167
    White House, 173
Folk music collection, 63, 68
Folsom, Frances, 94
Ford, Betty, 114
Ford, Gerald R., 22, 100, 104, 125
Ford Model T, 147
Ford's Theatre, 137
Fordyce and Hanby Associates, 122
Forrestal, James, Building, 122
Fortune magazine, 48
Foster, William Dewey, 126
Foucault pendulum, 147

France, 57, 65
Frank Grad and Sons, 122
Franklin, Benjamin, 62, 103, 139
Fraser, James Earle, 72
Freer, Charles Lang, 137
Freer Gallery of Art, 137
French, Daniel Chester, 140
French Second Empire style, 109, 153
Frohman, Philip Hubert, 158-159
Fulton, Robert, 65

Garden Cafe, National Gallery of Art, 148
Garden Room, White House, 90
Gardens. *See* Arboretums and gardens
Garfield, James A., 31, 94, 134, 150
Garland, Judy, 147
General Services Administration, 125, 127
"Genius of America" (Persico), 17
Geological Survey, U.S., 124
George VI (king of England), 96
Georgia marble, 72, 139, 140
Germany, 65
Gettysburg Address (Lincoln), 63, 140
Giant Bible of Mainz, 62
Gibbon, Edward, 65
Gilbert, Cass, 71, 82
Gilbert, Cass, Jr., 82
"Ginevra de' Benci" (da Vinci), 144
Girard College, 17
Glossary of congressional terms, 177-183
Gold Room, White House, 90
Gotelli Dwarf Conifer Collection, National Arboretum, 156
Government Printing Office, 68
Graham, Anderson, Probst, and White, 126
Gramm-Rudman-Hollings Deficit Reduction Act, 179-180
Grand Foyer, Kennedy Center, 139
Grand Salon, Renwick Gallery, 153
Grant, Ulysses S., 95, 98, 129
Great Hall, Library of Congress, 58, 59, 67
Great Hall, National Building Museum, 143
Great Hall, Supreme Court Building, 71, 72
Great Seal of the United States, 126, 143
Greece, 65
Greek (classical) revival style, 17, 110, 124, 127, 129
Greene, Nathanael, 29

193

Index

Green Room, White House, 92, 94
Grotius, Hugo, 73
Guerin, Jules, 140
Gutenberg Bible, 55, 62, 67

Hadfield, George, 12, 13
Hall, Asaph, 156
Hallet, Stephen M., 11-13
Hall of Nations, Kennedy Center, 139
Hall of Presidents, National Portrait Gallery, 151
Hall of States, Kennedy Center, 139
Hammurabi (lawgiver), 29, 73
Handicapped access. *See* specific buildings
Hanks, Nancy, Center, 152-153
Harbeson, John, 47
Harbeson, Hough, Livingston, and Larson, 47
Harding, Warren G., 31, 94, 104
Harrison, Benjamin, 86, 105
Harrison, Caroline, 91
Harrison, William Henry, 94
Hart, Frederick, 157
Hart, Philip A., 52
Hart Senate Office Building, 45, 48, 52-53, 61
Haupt, Enid A., Garden, 137-138
Haupt, Enid Annenberg, 138
Haydn manuscripts, 63
Hayes, Rutherford B., 22, 95, 103, 104
Health and Human Services Department (HHS), 122, 125
Henry, Joseph, 65
Herodotus, 65
Higgins, Daniel P., 139
Hirshhorn, Joseph H., 138
Hirshhorn Museum and Sculpture Garden, 138, 148
"History of Labor in America, The" (Beal), 125
His Whiskers (goat), 105
Hoban, James, 11-13, 85, 86, 92, 94, 98
Homer (Greek poet), 65
Homer, Winslow, 147
Hoover, Herbert C., 31, 104, 109
Hoover, Herbert Clark, Building, 118-119
Hoover, J. Edgar, Building, 125, 136
Hope Diamond, 150
Hopper, Edward, 138, 147
Hornaday, William Temple, 152
Hors d'Oeuvrerie cafe, Kennedy Center, 148
House Annex 1, 46

House Annex 2, 46
House of Commons, 31
House of Representatives
  activities. *See* Congressional activities
  office buildings. *See* Congressional office buildings
  quarters. *See* Capitol building
Housing and Urban Development, Department of (HUD), 122-123
Hughes, Charles Evans, 74, 82
Hull, Cordell, 111
Humphrey, Hubert H., Building, 122
Hunt, Richard Morris, 156
Huxtable, Ada Louise, 50-51

Ice Cream Parlour, National Museum of American History, 149
Ickes, Harold, 123-124
Immigration and Naturalization Service, 125
Inaugural addresses, 140
Inaugural balls and receptions, 79, 134, 143, 147
Inaugural sites, 4, 9, 16, 22, 23
Independence Hall, Philadelphia, 77
India granite, 157
Indiana limestone, 25, 139, 140
Indian arts and crafts shop, Interior Dept., 124
Indian studies, 147
Indian Treaty Room, Old Executive Office Building, 110
Ingersoll, Charles J., 79
Insect Zoo, National Museum of Natural History, 150
Interior Department, 18, 117, 123-124
Internal Revenue Service, 129
International architectural style, 123
International Center, S. Dillon Ripley Center, 154
Iran-contra hearings, 36, 51
Islam, 65
Italian marble, 57, 71-72, 127, 139, 144
Italy, 65, 127

Jackson, Andrew, 22, 25, 97
  Treasury building site selection, 3, 127
  White House residence, 86, 95, 96, 103
James, Daniel "Chappie," 134
Japan, 111
Javits, Jacob K., 40
Jefferson, Thomas, 22, 25, 62, 92, 138
  artistic renderings of, 29, 103, 139, 143
  Capitol construction involvement, 12-14

Index

library of, 55
White House residence, 94, 103
Jefferson Building, Library of Congress, 56-58, 66, 67, 71
Jefferson Memorial, 138-139
Jenkins Heights, 15
Jenkins Hill, 4
Jennewein, C. Paul, 124
John (king of England), 73
John Bull locomotive, 147
Johnson, Adelaide, 29
Johnson, Andrew, 127
Johnson, Lady Bird, 100, 104
Johnson, Luci, 101
Johnson, Lynda, 101
Johnson, Lyndon B., 31
Johnston, J. Bennett, 35
Journal (House), 34
Judea, 65
Judicial branch, 5-6. *See also* Supreme Court entries
Judiciary Act of 1789, 75
Judiciary Square, 5-6
Juliana (queen of Netherlands), 96
Julliard String Quartet, 62, 67
Justice Department, 117, 124-125
Justinian (lawgiver), 73

Kefauver committee hearings, 36
Kennedy, Caroline, 101, 105
Kennedy, Jacqueline, 88, 91, 94, 98-100, 104
Kennedy, Jacqueline, Garden, White House, 90, 104
Kennedy, John F., 31, 90, 110, 139
  gravesite, 134
  inauguration, 23
  White House residence, 94, 98, 100, 102-104
Kennedy, John F., Center for the Performing Arts, 108, 127, 139, 148
Kennedy, John F., Jr., 103
Kennedy, Robert F., 134
Kent, James, 65
Kline, Franz, 147

Labor Department, 125
Lafayette, Marquis de, 17
Langley, Samuel, 152
Langley Theater, Air and Space Museum, 141
Lane, Samuel, 16
Latrobe, Benjamin Henry, 13-14, 16, 21, 25, 78-79

Law Library, Library of Congress, 66
Lebanon, 106
Lee, Robert E., 133
Lee-Custis mansion, 134
Legislative process, 170, 177-183
Legislature quarters. *See* Capitol building; Congressional office buildings
L'Enfant, Pierre Charles, 3-6, 10, 97, 133
L'Enfant Plaza, 3
Leutze, Emanuel, 26
Librarians of Congress, 56, 66
Libraries, Old Executive Office Building, 110
Library, Supreme Court Building, 74
Library, White House, 92
Library Committee, Joint, 42, 66
Library of Congress, 55-68
  buildings, 56-62
  Great Hall, 58, 59, 67
  history, 9, 20, 55-56
  Kennedy Center library, 139-140
  location, 3, 56, 57, 71, 79
  main reading room, 57, 58, 65-67
  outstanding treasures, 55, 62-63
  service to Congress, 66
  service to public, 66-68
  type and scope of holdings, 61-64
  visitors information, 57
Lin, Maya Ying, 157
Lincoln, Abraham, 19-20, 31, 147
  artistic renderings, 25, 29, 103
  assassination, 137, 150
  collected papers, 63
  White House residence, 93-94, 96, 97
Lincoln, Mary Todd, 97, 98, 127
Lincoln Bedroom, White House, 88, 96-97
Lincoln catafalque, 31
Lincoln Gallery, National Museum of American Art, 147
Lincoln Memorial, 3, 140-141, 156
Lincoln Museum, Ford's Theatre, 137
Lincoln Sitting Room, White House, 96, 97
Lincoln Suite, White House, 96-98
Lindbergh, Charles A., 141
Little, Henry B., 159
Livingston, Robert R., 139
Lobbying, origin of term, 43
Long's Tavern, 79
Longworth, Alice Roosevelt, 99-100
Longworth, Nicholas, 46
Longworth House Office Building, 45, 46, 48

195

Index

Louis, Joe, 133
Louis, Saint, 73
Louisiana Purchase, 63
Lycurgus (lawgiver), 73
Lynn, David, 82

Macaroni (pony), 105
McCloskey, Matthew H., 47
McCloskey & Co., 47
McCune, Wesley, 72
Mace, 25, 31-33
McKim, Mead, and White, 93
McKinley, William, 31, 94
MacLeish, Archibald, 56
McPherson, Sandra, 68
Madison, Dolley, 86, 93, 95, 98
Madison, James, 22, 55, 60, 62, 143
   White House residence, 93, 94, 100
Madison Memorial Building, Library of Congress, 57, 58, 60-62, 66
Magna Carta, 55, 143
Magruder, Patrick, 56
Majority leader, 180
Majority whip, 180
Maltby Building, 44
Management and Budget, Office of, 109
Map Room, White House, 92
Maps. *See* Floor plans and maps
"Maquette for Mountains and Clouds" (Calder), 53
Marshall, George C., 134
Marshall, John, 73, 74, 78
Mars satellites, 156
Martiny, Philip, 58
Maryland, 4, 19
Maryland marble, 158
Mason, George, 63
Massachusetts, 19
Master Clock, Naval Observatory, 156
Matisse, Henri, 138, 145
Meehan, John S., 56
Meigs, Montgomery C., 18-19, 143
Mellon, A. W., Educational and Charitable Trust, 144
Mellon, Andrew W., 144
Mellon, Andrew W., Foundation, 145
Mellon, Paul, 53, 144
Mellon, Rachel Lambert, 104
Menes (lawgiver), 73
Metro subway, 3, 57
Meyers, Harold B., 48
Michelangelo Buonarroti, 65
Middle Ages, 65
Mills, Robert, 127, 158

Minnesota granite, 139
Minton tile, 25, 110
Mohammed (prophet), 73
Mondale, Joan, 114-115
Mondale, Walter F., 114-115
Monet, Claude, 90
Monroe, James, 16, 22, 63, 79, 94, 95
"Morning on the Seine" (Monet), 90
Moses, 65, 73
Mott, Lucretia, 30
Mount St. Alban, 158
Mount Vernon, 30, 31
Mozart manuscripts, 63
Mullett, Alfred Bult, 109, 129
Mumford, L. Quincy, 56, 58
Murals. *See* Paintings, portraits, and murals
Murphy, Audie, 134
Music manuscripts, 63

Nassif, David, 127
Nassif Building, 127
National Aeronautics and Space Administration, 121
National Air and Space Museum, 4, 141-142, 148
National Airport, 106
National Aquarium, 119, 142, 148
National Aquarium Society, 142
National Arboretum, 155-156
National Archives and Records Administration, 62, 142-143
National Bonsai Collection, National Arboretum, 156
National Building Museum, 143-144
National Endowment of the Arts, 153
National Gallery of Art, 144-145, 148-149
National Geographic Society, 127, 145-146
National Herb Garden, National Arboretum, 156
National Industrial Recovery Act, 82
National Intelligencer, 80
National Military Command Center, 108, 120
National Museum of African Art, 137, 146
National Museum of American Art, 146-147, 149, 151, 153
National Museum of American History, 134, 147, 149, 150
National Museum of Health and Medicine, 150

Index

National Museum of Natural History, 149, 150
National Park Service, 103, 139, 140
National Park System Advisory Board, 117
National Portrait Gallery, 147, 151
National Security Council, 109
National War College, 121
National Zoological Park, 149, 152
Naturalist Center, Museum of Natural History, 151
Naval Observatory, 113, 121, 156-157
Navy Department, 109, 117,125
Necksei-Lipozc Bible, 62
Neoclassical style, 117, 118, 126
Nevada, 29
New Executive Office Building, 111
New Mexico, 29
Newton, Isaac, 65
New York Chamber Soloists, 67
New York City, 4, 76-77
New York Statesman, 80-81
New York Times, 50
1976 Bicentennial, 14, 24, 33, 41, 68, 125
Nixon, Patricia, 94, 100, 104
Nixon, Richard, 24, 36, 100, 102
Nixon, Tricia, 104
North Dakota, 29

Occupational Safety and Health Administration, 125
Octagon Room, Renwick Gallery, 153
Odhecaton, 63
Office of. *See* specific office names
Old Executive Office Building (OEOB), 109-111, 117, 125, 129
Old Patent Office Building, 151
Old Post Office, 149, 152-153
Olmsted, Frederick Law, 4, 20-21, 152
O'Neill, Thomas P., Jr., 36
Opera House, Kennedy Center, 139
Oral argument, 73, 76
Otis Historical Archives, National Museum of Health and Medicine, 150
Oval Office, White House, 85, 88, 103

Page program, 37-40
Page Residence Hall, 39
Paintings, portraits, and murals
   Capitol, 25-29
   Interior Dept., 123
   Justice Dept., 125
   Labor Dept., 125

Library of Congress, 58, 65
National Archives, 143
White House, 90, 91, 98
See also Art galleries
Parade magazine, 60
Paris Opera House, 57, 72
Parklawn Building, 122
Parliamentarians, 181
Patent Corridor, Capitol, 28
Patent Office, 15, 42
Patent Pending Cafe, National Museum of American Art, 149
Patronage appointments, 37
Paul, Saint, 65
Pauline Wayne (cow), 103
Pavilion, Old Post Office, 149
"Peacock Room" (Whistler), 137
Peale, Charles Wilson, 25, 147
Peale, Rembrandt, 25
Pearl Harbor attack, 111
Peary, Robert E., 133
Pei, I. M., and Architects, 144
Pelz, Paul J., 56
Pennell, Joseph, 63
Pension Bureau, 143
Pentagon and Defense Department, 108, 117, 119-122, 123
Performing Arts Library, Kennedy Center, 139-140
Perkins, Frances, 125
Perot, H. Ross, 143
Pershing, John J., 134
Persico, Luigi, 17
Petersen, William, 137
Petersen House, 137
Petrucci (publisher), 63
Philadelphia, 4, 77-78, 96
Philadelphia Centennial Exposition (1876), 33, 42, 134
Photographs permitted. *See* specific buildings and museums
Phyfe, Duncan, 94
Picasso, Pablo, 138
Piccirilli brothers, 140
Pickford, Mary, Theater, 67
Pierce, Franklin, 18
Pilgrim Observatory Gallery, National Cathedral, 159
Pitts, Mebane, Phelps, and White, 125
Plato, 65
Plaza Cafe, Hirshhorn Museum, 148
Pollock, Jackson, 145
Poor, Henry Varnum, 123
Pope, John Russell, 138, 142,144

197

Index

Poplar Point Nursery, 11, 42
Postal Service, U.S., 153
Post Office Department, 15
Potomac River, 3, 4
Powhatan Indians, 4
Preservation of the White House, Committee for, 88, 90
Presidential papers, 55, 63
President of the Senate, 181
President pro tempore of the Senate, 38, 181
Presidents, list of, 174-175
President's Commission on Fine Arts, 110, 124-125
President's Dining Room, White House, 99-100
"Progress of Civilization, The" (Crawford), 29
Pryor, David, 40
Public Health Service, 122
Public Works Administration, 123
"Puritans on Their Way to America" (Weiers), 26
Putnam, Herbert, 56, 64

Quayle, Dan, 115
Quayle, Marilyn, 115
Queens' Bedroom, White House, 88, 96
Queens' Suite, White House, 96

Racial segregation, 74
Rankin, Kellog, and Crane, 117
Rauschenberg, Robert, 147
Rayburn, Sam, 23, 46, 47
Rayburn House Office Building, 44-51, 60, 61
Reading rooms, Library of Congress, 57, 58, 65-67
Reagan, Nancy, 88, 91, 98, 100
Reagan, Ronald, 110
  inaugural site, 4, 22
  White House residence, 88, 98, 100, 103
Recreational facilities
  Hart Building, 52, 53
  Rayburn Building, 50
  White House, 104-105
Red Room, White House, 92, 94-95
Rembrandt van Rijn, 144
Renwick, James, Jr., 153, 154
Renwick Gallery, 136, 147, 153-154
Republican Conference, House, 45
Resolute desk, 103

Restaurants. *See* Cafeterias and restaurants
Rhode Island, 29
Ripley, S. Dillon, 154
Ripley, S. Dillon, Center, 137, 154
Roach, John Charles, 28
Robb, E. Donald, 159
Robbins, Warren M., Library, 146
Robinson, Boardman, 125
Rockart, John R., 82
Rockefeller, Margaretta (Happy), 114
Rockefeller, Nelson, 114
Rodin, Auguste, 138
Roe v. Wade, 74
Rogers, Isaiah, 129
Rogers, Randolph, 30
Rome, 32, 65
Roof Terrace Restaurant, Kennedy Center, 148
Roosevelt, Eleanor, 90, 95, 105
Roosevelt, Franklin D., 22, 94, 125
  presidency, 76, 82, 123, 144
  White House residence, 90-92, 98, 100, 102, 103
Roosevelt, Quentin, 105
Roosevelt, Theodore
  presidency, 46, 158
  White House residence, 86, 90, 92, 94, 97, 102, 104, 105
Roosevelt Room, White House, 102
Rose Garden, White House, 104
Rosenwald, Lessing J., 63
Ross, Robert, 14
Rotunda, Capitol (main), 20
  art work in, 9, 17, 25, 26
  crypt, 30-31
  dimensions, 15, 19
  inaugural site, 22
Rotunda, Capitol (small Senate), 16, 25
Rubin, Joseph, 67
Russell, Richard Brevard, 51
Russell Senate Office Building, 45, 48, 51
Russo-Japanese War, 102
Ryder, Albert Pinkham, 147

Sackler, Arthur M., 154
Sackler, Arthur M., Gallery, 137, 154
St. Paul's Cathedral, 19
St. Peter's Basilica, 19
Schubert manuscripts, 63
Scobee, Dick, 133
Scruggs, Jan, 157
Secretary of the Senate, 182
Secret Service, 90, 105

Index

Security and communications
   Capitol, 37
   White House, 85, 105-108
Segreti, Anthony J., 159
"Self-Portrait" (Rembrandt), 144
Senate
   activities. *See* Congressional activities
   office buildings. *See* Congressional office buildings
   quarters. *See* Capitol building
Sergeant-at-arms, 32, 33
Shakespeare, William, 65
Sherman, Roger, 139
Simon, Louis A., 126
Situation Room, White House, 108
Skylab Orbital Workshop, 141
Slave labor, 13
Smith, Michael, 133
Smith, Robert C., 159
Smithmeyer, John L., 56
Smithsonian Institution, 3, 30
   Anacostia Museum, 133
   Air and Space Museum, 141-142
   Arthur M. Sackler Gallery, 154
   Arts and Industries Building, 134
   Castle/Information Center, 154-155
   dining areas, 148-149
   Enid A. Haupt Garden, 137-138
   Freer Gallery of Art, 137
   hours of operation, 133
   Museum of African Art, 137, 146
   Museum of American Art, 146-147
   Museum of American History, 134, 147, 150
   Museum of Natural History, 150-151
   National Portrait Gallery, 147, 151
   Renwick Gallery, 153-154
   S. Dillon Ripley Center, 154
   Zoological Park, 152
Smoking permitted. *See* specific buildings and museums
Smoot, Reed, 109
Social Security Administration, 122
Solarium, White House, 101-102
Solomon (lawgiver), 73
Solon (lawgiver), 65, 73
Somervell, Brehon B., 119
South Building, Agriculture Dept., 117, 118
Spanish marble, 71
Speaker of the House, 33, 34, 36, 182
"Spirit of St. Louis," 141
Spofford, Ainsworth R., 56
Stanton, Elizabeth Cady, 30

Star-Spangled Banner, 147
Star Wars, 61
State, War, and Navy Building, 109, 125, 129
State Department, 108, 109, 117, 119, 125-126
State Department Library, 110
State Dining Room, White House, 92, 95
State of the Union messages, 36
Statuary Hall, Capitol, 9, 14, 21, 29, 33
Statue of Freedom, Capitol, 15, 20, 30
Statue of Liberty, 42
Statues and sculptures
   Capitol, 29-30
   Library of Congress, 58
Stephenson, John G., 56
Stewart, J. George, 23, 24, 47, 48, 51, 60
Stone, Edward Durell, 127, 139
Stone, Harlan Fiske, 74
Stradivari, Antonio, 55, 62
Stradivari instruments, 55, 61, 62, 67
Stuart, Gilbert, 25, 86, 93, 147
Studds, Gerry E., 40
"Substantial federal question," 75
Subway. *See* Metro subway; Tunnels and subway system
Sully, Thomas, 25
Supreme Court
   early quarters, 5-6, 9, 14, 16, 21, 76-82
   number of justices, 75-76
   role and procedures, 74-76
   wearing of robes, 78
Supreme Court building
   construction history, 82
   court's move to, 71
   design and layout, 71-74
   location, 3, 6, 16, 71
   visitors information, 73

Taft, William Howard, 22, 31, 82, 103, 133
Taney, Roger B., 74
Telephone exhibit, 147
Telephone system, 108
Telescope sites, 156-157
Television coverage of congressional activities, 33-37
Ten Commandments tableau, 73
Tennessee, 71, 157
Tennessee marble, 57, 140, 144, 145
Terrace Cafe, National Gallery of Art, 148-149
Terrace Theatre, Kennedy Center, 139
Theatre Lab, Kennedy Center, 139

Index

Thornton, William, 10-14, 21
Tiber Creek, 5, 118
Time, telephone recording, 157
Time magazine cover collection, 151
Tobacco leaf capitals, 16, 25
Tomb of the Unknowns, 134
Tour information. *See* specific buildings and museums
Transportation Department, 127
Treasury Annex, 129
Treasury Department building, 3, 15, 106, 110, 117, 119, 127-129
Treaty Room, White House, 88, 96, 98
Truman, Harry S, 109
   White House residence, 86, 88, 95, 96, 98, 99, 103, 104
Truman balcony, White House, 88, 98
Trumbull, John, 17, 25-26
Tuchman, Barbara W., 68
Tunnels and subway system
   Capitol and office buildings, 44, 48-49, 51
   Library of Congress, 57
Twain, Mark, 109
Tyler, John, 98

Underwood, Gilbert S., 126
Union Station, 3, 155
University of Virginia, 138
U.S. Marshals Service, 125
Utah, 29

Vatican, 72
Vaughan, Henry, 158
Vedder, Elihu, 58
Vermeil Room, White House, 90
Vermont, 157
Vermont marble, 72, 139, 144
Veterans Administration, 129
Veterans Affairs, Department of, 129
Vice president
   list, 174-175
   office, 109
   residence, 113-115
Victoria (queen of England), 103
Victorian Ice Cream Parlour, National Museum of American History, 149
Vietnam Veterans Memorial, 3, 4, 157
Vietnam War, 36
Virginia, 5, 13, 31
Virginia bill of rights, 63
Visitors information
   Capitol, 11
   Congressional office buildings, 45

Library of Congress, 57
Old Executive Office Building, 111
Pentagon, 119
State Dept., 119
Supreme Court building, 73
Treasury Dept., 119
White House, 87
See also specific buildings and museums
Von Eckhardt, Wolf, 61-62

Walter, Thomas Ustick, 17-21, 43, 129
Walter Reed Army Medical Center, 121, 150
War Department, 18, 109, 110, 117, 125
Warnecke, John Carl, 111
Warnecke, John Carl, and Associates, 53
Warneke, Heinz, 123
War of 1812, 9, 10, 14, 79, 86
Warren, Earl, 74
War Risk Building, 129
Washington, George, 26, 96, 103
   capital city planning, 3-5, 139
   Capitol planning, 10-12, 123
   collected papers, 63
   Gilbert Stuart portrait, 25, 86, 93
   inaugural sites, 22
   tomb, 30-31
   White House planning, 85, 97
Washington, John A., 31
Washington, Martha, 30
Washington, D.C.
   Capitol Hill plan, 163
   city plan, 3-6
   Supreme Court early quarters, 78-82
Washington Monument, 3, 127, 158
Washington-Moscow hot line, 108, 120
Washington National Cathedral, 158-159
Washington Post, 45, 61
Watergate hearings, 36, 51
Watterston, George, 56
Webster, Daniel, 25, 100
Weiers, Robert W., 26
Weinman, Adolph A., 73, 139
West, J. B., 99
West Building, National Gallery of Art, 144, 148
West Front, Capitol, 9, 10, 21-25
Westminster Abbey, 153
West Sitting Hall, White House, 99
West Wing, White House, 85, 89, 102-103
West Wing Reception Room, White House, 102

200

Index

Whistler, James McNeill, 137, 147
Whistler items collection, 63
White, Alexander, 78
White, George M., 24, 52
White House, 85-108
   construction and restorations, 11, 12, 15, 85-86, 88
   East Wing and ground floor, 90-92
   first or state floor, 92-96
   floor plans, 173
   general description, 85, 89-90
   grounds, 103-105
   historic landmark designation, 117
   inaugural site, 22
   location, 3, 85
   second and third floors, 88, 96-102
   security and communications, 85, 105-108
   visitors information, 87
   West Wing, 102-103
White House Historical Association, 87, 90
White House Law Library, 110
White House Library and Research Center, 110
White House Office, 109
Whitmer, David J., 120
Whitney, Eli, 147

Whittall, Gertrude Clark, Foundation, 67
Wilhelmina (queen of Netherlands), 96
Wilkes, Charles, 42
Wilson, Edith Bolling, 90-91
Wilson, Ellen Axson, 104
Wilson, Woodrow, 13, 22, 63, 91, 97, 103
Wilson, Woodrow, International Center for Scholars, 155
Wizard of Oz, 147
Women's suffrage memorial, 29-30
Wood, Waddy B., 123
World War II, 21
Wouk, Herman, 68
Wright brothers' flyer, 141
Wright Place Restaurant, Air and Space Museum, 148
Wyatt and Nolting, 129

Yellow Oval Room, White House, 88, 96, 98
York and Sawyer, 118
Young, Ammi B., 129
Young, Cliff, 26, 28
Young, John R., 56

Zantzinger, Clarence, 124
Zoo, 149, 152
Zumwalt, Elmo R., 113

201

FUNDERBURG LIBRARY
MANCHESTER COLLEGE